SOMEONE TO LOVE, SOMEONE LIKE YOU

SOMEONE TO LOVE, SOMEONE LIKE YOU

Poems of Divine and Human Love

TERRY A. VELING

Foreword by John Honner

RESOURCE *Publications* • Eugene, Oregon

SOMEONE TO LOVE, SOMEONE LIKE YOU
Poems of Divine and Human Love

Copyright © 2020 Terry A. Veling. All rights reserved. Except for brief quotations in critical publications or reviews, no part of this book may be reproduced in any manner without prior written permission from the publisher. Write: Permissions, Wipf and Stock Publishers, 199 W. 8th Ave., Suite 3, Eugene, OR 97401.

Resource Publications
An Imprint of Wipf and Stock Publishers
199 W. 8th Ave., Suite 3
Eugene, OR 97401

www.wipfandstock.com

PAPERBACK ISBN: 978-1-5326-9060-0
HARDCOVER ISBN: 978-1-5326-9061-7
EBOOK ISBN: 978-1-5326-9062-4

Manufactured in the U.S.A.   01/20/20

To my four sons

To Joel
To Simon
To Reuben
To Asher

I thank God each time I think of you

Abba

You know it never has been easy
Whether you do or you do not resign
Whether you travel the breadth of extremities
Or stick to some straighter line

—Joni Mitchell

Contents

Foreword by John Honner | ix

Preface | xiii

Prologue: Poetry is Essential to the Human Spirit | xv

1   In the Beginning | 1

2   Resistance | 31

3   Time, Death, Memory | 69

4   Singularity | 106

5   Natural Lover | 128

6   Desire | 161

7   You/Divinity | 200

Bibliography | 233

Foreword

The pioneering township of Berry is a couple of hours by car south of Sydney. In my bare-foot holidays I loved to explore the Berry Tip, as it was known, because it was a treasure trove of petrol drums, used timber, fencing wire, old sofas, and all the materials I needed to create a magical raft on the nearby Crooked River.

Almost fifty years later I came to live in Berry. While the Tip had been transformed into "The Berry Recycling and Waste Facility," and while pilfering was now forbidden, the manager of the facility—his name was Col—had set aside a small shed for items which were too good to throw away and could be purchased by the general public.

Because I was a dutiful recycler, Col and I got to trust each other. When I'd completed sorting my cardboard, building waste and greenery, I would stop by his shed. There were old vinyl records, golf clubs, clocks, scooters, surfboards, exercise machines, and plenty of books. On my very last visit I spied *The Redress of Poetry*, by Seamus Heaney, a collection of his lectures when he was professor of poetry at Oxford. The book was published in 1995. Later that year Heaney was awarded the Nobel Prize for Literature. The book was in perfect condition. This was a treasure.

How much for this?, I asked Col. What's it about?, he replied. It's about poetry, I said. You can have it for nothing, he said. In one sense Col was right: you can have poetry for nothing.

Terry Veling has a constant refrain in his Prologue: "Poetry is essential to the human spirit . . . Poetic acts happen all the time in life." Among his collection of treasures is a quote from Jacques Maritain: "Poetry is engaged in the free creativity of God's spirit." You can have poetry for nothing.

There is, however, a personal cost. Poetry can never be a self-aggrandising flourish. Rather, Terry writes, "it is both revealing and sacrificing." He confesses that he rarely shares his poetry and that he never really exposes himself, yet here he places his life in our hands. These poems constitute a spiritual journal. They are not abstractions. They are to be treated with tenderness.

Each poem comes on a new page. For a time I wondered about this. It seemed indulgent. A waste of paper. But then I realised I was being like Judas, complaining about Mary of Bethany's extravagance in anointing Jesus' feet: he was thinking about the cost of the perfume instead of marvelling at the lesson in generosity. By giving each poem a page, Terry shows a profound generosity and reverence for the gift of a poem, for the free creativity of God's spirit. Crowding the poems together on a single page would be like displaying several paintings in the one frame. The blank space around each poem on each page should remind the reader to pause, to allow the poem to free her from the bounds of time and space.

Seamus Heaney's book, *The Redress of Poetry*, is a set of reflections on the ways that poetry redresses falsehood and redresses disorder: "It is the imagination pressing back against the pressure of reality."[1] He delights in an old Eskimo woman who had been asked why all the songs sung by her tribe were so short. Her reply: "Because we know so much."[2] This does not mean that poetry simplifies issues, but that it "brings human existence into a fuller life."[3] This is the redress of poetry.

Terry has a gift for wonder and gratitude. He reminds us that poetry is on the side of life. He lives in a physical and colloquial world with disarming simplicity. Instead of sentimentality, cliché and pretension you will find creative imagination, incisive reflection, gentle humour. These are poems of wisdom, about a life lived in the body and in nature, about faith, hope and love, about time, suffering and death. There are lines that describe his quest for both a poem and a way of life, like "Aphorism":

> How do you write an aphorism?
> You keep cutting it back and back
> until very little remains
> except the essential.

This approach leads to memorable aphorisms, offering Rumi-like wisdom, as in "Do What You Love":

---

1. Heaney, *The Redress of Poetry*, 1.
2. Heaney, *The Redress of Poetry*, 175.
3. Heaney, *The Redress of Poetry*, xvii.

> Do what you love
> This is your best antidote
> to doing what you hate.

And it should come as no surprise that the shortest poem in the collection—"The Wind"—is also the most beautiful, the most sensual, the most arresting and the most spiritual:

> The wind is the most naked body.

There are several longer poems that have to be read out loud. Then you will find the melody and the rhythm, and be drawn into the slow voicing of an inevitable drama, as in "Recluse":

> You haven't gone out lately?
> No, I've been caught
> trapped
> bound
> tied
> constrained
> confined
> caged
> roped
> hung
> sunk
> shipwrecked.

There are poems about faith, resurrection, and God. And above all there are poems of body and heart, poems of love. Love is physical, immediate, external, eternal. Some of the love poems are romantic and visionary at the same time, as in "When I was Young":

> When I was young
> you made me feel that
> nothing would be perfect
> without you
>
> Now I am old
> very little has changed.

Foreword

Finally, do not allow yourself to become too serious when reading these poems. After the long Prologue, the first poem is called "At Last"! There is a smiling contrast between the colloquialism of the poems and the solemn prose of the Prologue. Both, however, point to the same insight, as Terry puts it, that "everything ordinary is laden with inspirational possibility . . . Thus the finite is to be treasured as the honored place where the infinite comes to pass."

I found the *The Redress of Poetry* among the finite treasures of the Berry Tip. Terry's poems remind me to continue to treasure the finite as the place where life can be lived to the full and the infinite does come to pass. And it costs nothing.

—JOHN HONNER

Preface

A few years ago Mary and I had the opportunity to purchase a sixteen acre bush property in the hinterland of the Sunshine Coast, north of Brisbane. We have a small caravan and a couple of tents on the property that we affectionately call "the land." We spend many of our weekends there enjoying the natural beauty of the bush, the birds and the stars.

It was during these times on the land that I began sorting and editing my many notebooks of poetry, spanning a couple of decades of musings, scribblings or "inklings"—to borrow that wonderful expression of the literary discussion group that C.S. Lewis and J.R.R. Tolkien belonged to. As an academic, I found this process liberating, connecting again with nature and soul, rather than the often heady world of academia. At first, I wasn't concerned whether anyone might read the poems I was cataloguing and editing. Yet, I have always thought that writing should not be "wasted"—rather, it is a gift meant to be shared.

Publishing poetry, however, is a hard sell. It is one of the most personal forms of communication, not made for a mass market. There are very few who write poetry with a view to a large readership. Rather, much like the older genre of the "diary," poetry is the intimate expression of thoughts and feelings. It is the embodiment of singular human experience. Some poems speak intimately, others feel distant. There is little that is entertaining or solely literary about poetry. Rather, poetry is the secret labor of the soul.

This volume consists of a mix of poetry and prose.[1] It begins with an opening essay that seeks to convey the vital connection between poetry and the human spirit. This is followed by seven sections of poetry, each of which have their own small prose introductions, covering themes such as desire, time, memory, resistance, natural love and divinity.

---

1. As an Australian writer, I have kept the poetry with its original British/Australian spelling. Some of the poems have appeared in previous publications. See Veling, *Spirial-Bound Poetry* and "Poetic Licence."

Preface

Publishing poetry is not an easy thing. For a start, it means exposing yourself, opening the "diaries" of your thoughts and feelings to others. Moreover, it means reading through pages and pages of old notebooks, trying to distil the essential. It is a personal journey and a personal expression, guided by only one hope, that somewhere and somehow it may touch a chord with another person, another soul.

I am convinced that the human spirit would be poorer without poetry, without art, without music. This is not to deny the vital role of the sciences. It is simply to say that the human spirit requires poetry, however unnoticed or unrecognized or unprofitable.

> For what shall it profit you
> if you should gain the whole world
> and lose your own soul?
> (Mark 8:36)

—TAV

Prologue
Poetry is Essential to the Human Spirit

"Go into your room, shut the door, and pray to the One who is in secret."
—See Matt 6:6

IN SEARCH OF POETRY

"I've been walking in a largely peach-colored, air-conditioned shopping mall," writes American poet Adrienne Rich. "I enter this mall rarely," she says. "But this time I am on a search."

> Inside, in a space the size of a small village, are clothing-chain outlets, fast-food parlors, stores selling computers and camcorders, stuffed animals, papier-mâché cactuses, mugs inscribed with names and mottoes, athletic shoes, real and plastic houseplants . . . The shops are stocked, to the inch, mostly with repetitions of identical merchandise, a plethora of tiny-choice variants on a single model; nothing here is eccentric, nothing bears the imprint of an individual maker . . .
>
> Here is a chain bookstore, stacked novels, computer manuals, intimacy manuals, parenting manuals, investment manuals, meditation manuals . . . I ask the young clerk at the register where the poetry is. He walks me toward the back of the store: "Those two shelves down there."[1]

---

1. Rich, *What is Found There*, 28–30.

Prologue

Adrienne Rich is on a search for poetry in the mall, yet all she manages to find are two small shelves buried at the back of the store. "Poetry is underneath," she says, and "awfully low 'down there.'" No one seems very interested in poetry, preferring the supposed reality of the shopping mall (which is full of copies, fakes and fabrications) to the reality of the poetic world, a world in which we may "poetically dwell."[2]

Rich laments the lack of poetry in the mall. She believes that poetry can stir the human imagination and help us re-describe and re-construct our world. The work of a poem "reminds you (for you have known, somehow, all along, maybe lost track) where and when and how you are living and might live—it is a wick of desire."[3]

Poetry can "break open locked chambers of possibility, restore numbed zones to feeling, recharge desire."[4] Poetry *makes* the world appear differently—as strange, as new, or even as freshly remembered, as though we had forgotten something essential. "Over so many millennia, so many cultures, humans have reached into preexisting nature and made art: to celebrate, to drive off evil, to nourish memory, to conjure the desired vision."[5]

The poetic word breaks open, energizes and restores, and it invites us to dwell in this newly opened, recharged and restored world.

"COMBINING THE LETTERS"

In order to discover the essentials of poetry there is nothing better for us to do than to learn from the "First Poet."[6]

> In the beginning God created the heavens and the earth. Now the earth was a formless void, there was darkness over the deep, and God's spirit hovered over the water. And God said . . . (Gen 1:1)

One of the names attributed to God by the rabbinic sages is "the One who spoke and the world came into being."[7] If God were to fall silent, creation would cease to exist. The prophet Isaiah puts it this way: "As the rain and the snow come down from heaven, and do not return until they have

---

2. Heidegger, *Poetry, Language, Thought*, 213 (adapted).
3. Rich, *What is Found There*, 241.
4. Rich, *What is Found There*, xiv.
5. Rich, *What is Found There*, 250.
6. Maritain, *Creative Intuition in Art and Poetry*, 112.
7. Heschel, *Heavenly Torah*, 6.

watered the earth, making it bring forth and sprout . . . so shall my word be that goes forth from my mouth; it shall not return to me empty, but it shall accomplish that which I purpose . . ." (55:10–11).

In the mystical tradition of Judaism, the Hebrew "aleph-bait" consists of the "letters of creation" by which God made heaven and earth.[8] "Twenty-two elemental letters," the Kabbalah says, "God engraved them, carved them, weighed them, permuted them, and transposed them, forming with them everything formed and everything destined to be formed."[9]

The Kabbalah tells us that we too can learn "to combine the letters by which heaven and earth were made."[10] It advises us to do good deeds and to engage in study, to combine the letters and receive the abundant flow of God's word:

> Take hold of ink, pen, and tablet. Realize that you are about to serve your God in joy. Begin to combine letters, a few or many, permuting and revolving them rapidly until your mind warms up. Delight in how they move and in what you generate by revolving them. When you feel within that your mind is very, very warm from combining the letters, and that through the combinations you understand new things . . . then you are ready to receive the abundant flow, arousing you again and again.[11]

When we begin "to combine the letters" we are seeking, as Paulo Freire suggests, to name the world. "To exist, humanly, is to *name* the world . . . Human beings are not built in silence, but in word, in work, in action-reflection."[12] There are many ways to name the world, which is more than simply placing "tags" on things, as though existence were simply waiting for us to label it. Rather, the very way we combine the letters and name the world creates the type of world that thereby comes into being. Moreover, it creates what we are able to see or fail to see; it creates the way we respond or fail to respond; it creates the limit or the expanse of our horizon—our "view of the world."

By recognizing the productive energy of the creative word, we are seeking to enliven our ability for seeing and naming the world which can too often be smothered in lazy familiarity or buried in unquestioned

---

8. Kushner, *The Book of Letters*.
9. Matt, *The Essential Kabbalah*, 102.
10. Kushner, *The Book of Letters*, 17.
11. Matt, *The Essential Kabbalah*, 103.
12. Freire, *Pedagogy of the Oppressed*, 61.

assumptions. Our conventional life, with its familiar patterns and objects, can sometimes become a husk that prevents anything fresh from coming in. It is in contrast to this dullness that Freire writes: "The naming of the world is an act of creation and recreation." It requires "an intense faith in humankind, faith in their power to make and remake, to create and re-create, faith in their vocation to be fully human."[13]

I often tell my students that there are only twenty-six letters in the English alphabet. When they go to the library, I ask them to consider that virtually every book among that vast array, stretching across centuries of writing, consists of no more than twenty-six letters. All that differs is the way the letters are combined, and these combinations—which can sometimes evoke whole worlds of meaning—are infinite in their creative possibilities. The same remains true for us today. Deep inside each person there are secret words ("combinations") waiting to be born. "There is a book which the finger of God writes in the heart of each person; no one can substitute for it."[14] We are in the world to love and name the world, and we too can "combine the letters" in such ways that our unique combinations may create and bring forth life.

Combining the letters is, of course, a literary metaphor, yet the metaphor can be extended. I remember looking at a beautifully constructed bridge with my brother who is a civil engineer. I saw the beauty of the bridge's shape and form, as did he, yet he also saw the physical laws and mathematical equations that were holding this bridge together. In other words, in the same way that we can combine the letters, we can also "combine the numbers" and, in like fashion, painters can "combine the colors," musicians can "combine the notes"—such that the elements of the universe can be combined in a variety of creative ways.

The creative intuition of the poet is attuned to the creativity of God, the "First Poet." The poet finds signs of heaven here on earth, seeing all things "in God." This is the way of the analogical imagination that sees everything as God's creation, lovingly crafted in God's image. This instinct or aspiration toward beauty and goodness draws us to consider the world as a "correspondence of heaven" or an "analogy of heaven." "Such is the supreme analogate of poetry," Jacques Maritain writes; "poetry is engaged in the free creativity of God's spirit."[15]

13. Freire, *Pedagogy of the Oppressed*, 62–63.
14. Leclercq, *The Love of Learning*, 260.
15. Maritain, *Creative Intuition in Art and Poetry*, 113.

CREATIVE INTUITION

Jewish philosopher Abraham Heschel notes that religion can sometimes be its own worst enemy. Rather than blame "secularism" for the demise of religion, Heschel says we need to look at the lack of creativity and relevance of our own faith traditions. "It is customary to blame secular science and antireligious philosophy for the eclipse of religion in modern society. It would be more honest to blame religion for its own defeats. Religion declined not because it was refuted, but because it became *irrelevant, dull, oppressive, insipid*. When faith is completely replaced by creed, worship by discipline, love by habit; when faith becomes an heirloom rather than *a living fountain*; when religion speaks only in the name of authority rather than with the voice of compassion—its message becomes meaningless."[16]

The ill health of religion is attributable to its dearth of creativity. Non-creative religious traditions lead to fundamentalism, irrationalism, and dogmatism—upon which the sources of war and conflict feed. Healthy religious traditions are attributable to the richness of creativity. Creative religious traditions lead to peace, healing, newfound wisdom—they draw on the sources of love and beauty.

In his work *Higher Education and the Human Spirit*, Bernard Meland argues that rational ways of knowing have tended to neglect deeper, intuitive ways of knowing, what he calls an *appreciative consciousness* or a "felt wisdom."[17] According to Meland, we live more deeply than we think. If we are to be faithful to lived experience, this "more deeply" should be reflected in our ways of knowing. Meland appeals to an appreciative consciousness that is attuned to humanity's way of apprehending the world through a sense of value, a sense of beauty, of feeling, affection, intuition—through moral, religious and aesthetic experience.

Paul Ricoeur suggests that the realm of the poetic and the symbolic "gives rise to thought."[18] Similarly, Bernard Lee notes that the production of concepts and ideas, which often appear to us as clear and distinct, are like thin abstractions of meaning that float on a vaster reserve of poetic and intuitive life. Religious perception, rather than being vague or indistinct, is often more in touch with the depth of human experience than the generalized abstractions of rational consciousness. "All systems of thought sooner

---

16. Heschel, *God in Search of Man*, 3 (italics mine).
17. Meland, "The Appreciative Consciousness."
18. Ricoeur, *The Symbolism of Evil*, 348.

or later exhaust the ability to illuminate experience."[19] Our rational ways of knowing have tended to neglect deeper, intuitive ways of knowing.

Most of us (in Western cultures) are the products of an Enlightenment consciousness that celebrates humanity's capacity for autonomous, critical and rational thought. There is no question that we need a critical consciousness. However, have we neglected to also develop an appreciative consciousness? While it is important to ask critical questions, it is also important to ask appreciative questions, to seek the Good. Goodness is everywhere to be found, even in situations where we might not expect to find it. It is God's gift to us. Yet we need an appreciative consciousness to open us to this goodness. This is neither naïveté nor rosy-colored romanticism. It requires much faith and a divinely attentive life to see the Good. I would even say, before you engage in critical inquiry, engage first in appreciative inquiry.

Catholic philosopher Jacques Maritain places creative intuition and appreciative inquiry at the heart of the poetic and artistic experience. Maritain does not oppose reason to intuition; rather he argues that in poetic experience, reason is freed from being purely logical and conceptual, and touches its deeper source that he calls "intuitive reason" (*intuitus rationis*). The poetic experience is a process of liberation from purely conceptual, logical, discursive reason. Yet it is by no means unreasonable if it is true that reason possesses a life that is deeper than its articulate logical life. In other words, we do not only have a rational and critical consciousness, we also have an intuitive and creative consciousness. Listen to Maritain:

> The spiritual life of the intellect is not engrossed by the preparation and engendering of its instruments of rational knowledge and by the production of concepts and ideas . . . Rather, there is still for the intellect another kind of life, which makes use of other resources and another reserve of vitality, and which is free; I mean free from the workings of rational knowledge and the disciplines of logical thought, free from the human actions to regulate and free from the laws of objective reality as to be known and acknowledged by science and discursive reason . . .
>
> This freedom is not freedom at random . . . it obeys an inner law of expansion and generosity, which carries it along toward the manifestation of the creativity of the spirit; and it is shaped and quickened by creative intuition. *Here it is, in this free life of the*

---

19. Lee, *Jesus and the Metaphors of God*, 184.

imagination, at the single root of the soul's powers, and in the unconscious life of the spirit, that poetry, I think, has its source."[20]

The creativity of the poet is his or her person *as person*—the creative self marked with the expressiveness proper to the human spirit. Poetry's *I* is not found in self-centered ego, but in the substantial depth of living and loving attentively, creatively and responsively. The creative self is both revealing and sacrificing. It dies to itself in order to live for the work. As such, egoism is the natural enemy of poetic activity. The very engagement of the poet is *for the sake of the work*.[21] What we receive from the poet is a gift of intellect and imagination, a new way of naming and living in the world.

POETIC ACTS

I recall celebrating the wedding of my son, Reuben, to Leesa. I witnessed their dedication to each other. I thought to myself, what more poetic act could there be than what I am witnessing now: an act of pure dedication. It is indeed filled with the poetry of love—as it should be on a wedding night—yet it is also filled with undying surrender and dedication. It is the ultimate poetic act. I give myself to you.

Dedicating our lives to one another is a sacrament in the Catholic tradition and a covenant in the Jewish tradition. The rabbis see this dedication encapsulated in the Song of Songs, of which Rabbi Akiba says: "If nothing had been given to us of Torah but the Song of Songs, it would have been a sufficient guide for human conduct."[22] Of all the scriptures, the Song is the most sacred of all. It reflects passion and desire—a "beautiful obsession"—not in any heedless way, but one that is filled with love and dedication.

Most of humanity's profound acts of saying "yes"—to another in marriage, to the call of religious life, to birthing and raising children, to a particular vocation or work—most of these avowals are not born from a purely logical choosing; rather, they are born of the creative intuition and secret labor of the soul. They are, at their heart, *poetic acts*. Maritain writes: "It is enough to think about the way in which our free decisions, when they are really free, are made, especially those decisions that commit our entire life—to realize that there exists a deep unconscious world of *intuitive*

---

20. Maritain, *Creative Intuition in Art and Poetry*, 110–11 (italics mine).
21. Maritain, *Creative Intuition in Art and Poetry*, 142–44.
22. Heschel, *Heavenly Torah*, 196 (citing *Song of Songs Zuta* 1:1).

Prologue

activity, for the intellect and the will, from which our acts emerge."[23] The bonds of our interpersonal and social relationships are ultimately founded in acts of dedication. Very little begins, or is sustained, without dedication.

Poetic experience is not a vague realm accessible only to a few esoteric or mystical souls. Poetic intuition and creativity is at work in a great variety of human disciplines—art, literature, science—all of which respond to the beauty and mystery of the world, the "divine milieu."[24] There is poetic intuition at work in science and mathematics; there is poetic intuition at work in the primary insights of philosophical thought; there is poetic intuition at work in the lives of saints and prophets—think of St. Francis' "Brother Sun and Sister Moon" or St. John of the Cross' "Dark Night of the Soul." Poetry is a secret labor that is at work in all of humanity's intellectual and spiritual gifts.

In every human endeavor of wonder and discovery, of commitment and dedication, there is a poetic spirit. Flying to the moon, for example, was surely not only a great scientific achievement, it was also a poetic act. Indeed, while orbiting the moon and seeing the earthrise for the very first time in human history, the crew of Apollo Eight sent a message back to earth on Christmas Eve, reciting the first ten verses of Genesis, "In the beginning God created the heavens and the earth. Now the earth was formless and void, and there was darkness over the deep . . ."

We often set up a false division between poetry and science, or between poetry and pragmatics, or between "uselessness" and "usefulness." That there is poetry in science seems to me a better thing to say than that poetry and science have no connection. What we need are poet-scientists, poet-thinkers, poet-practitioners. We need people who are inspired—inspired to question and explore, inspired to think and not simply reason, inspired to put into practice, not leaving things undone. Inspired acts are better than uninspired acts. This doesn't mean that ordinary actions don't count; it means that everything ordinary is laden with inspirational possibility.

I have an old copy of a book written by Thomas Merton in the nineteen-fifties, titled *Silence in Heaven: A Book of Monastic Life*. It is a splendid hard-cover volume that I purchased at a library book sale and its pages have a lovely musky, incense smell. In black and white photography, the book depicts the various works of the monks: tilling the land, working in

---

23. Maritain, *Creative Intuition in Art and Poetry*, 93–94.
24. Chardin, *The Divine Milieu*.

the laboratory, a kitchen with pots boiling, a leather workshop, a loom, an art studio, a monk with a finely detailed architectural drawing, monks bent over books in study, and monks in silent and communal prayer. All these activities bring together what Jean Leclercq calls "the love of learning and the desire for God."[25]

Poetic acts happen all the time in life. There are probably a million weddings happening around the globe even as I write. There are paintings being painted, poems being written, songs composed, discoveries made, goodness and beauty recreated. Poetry is essential to the human spirit. Poetry is not utilitarian action—reduced to pure "usefulness." Poetry is more akin to divine action— expanding into creativity. The poetic act is creative. It tends toward creation.

RE-IMAGINING OUR WORLD

We cannot approach poetry as something that is simply edifying, "for the sake of sheltered people."[26] Rather, when we come upon real poetry, we often encounter prophetic voices that unsettle conventional opinions and routines, that name realities and truths that many are either blind to see or don't want to be seen. Along with the analogical imagination, there is also the prophetic imagination. Dorothee Soelle, for example, notes that religious traditions have always included forms of prophetic resistance: "Whether it be withdrawal, renunciation, disagreement, divergence, dissent, reform, rebellion, or revolution, in all these there is a *No!* to the world as it exists now."[27]

Poetic art is not subservient, but eminently free to name things as they really are, no matter how disturbing or uncomfortable. Poetic art seeks to break down "social and utilitarian connotations, worn-out meanings, and habit." In poetry, we find an entrance "where everything is other than as usual."[28]

Poets and artists are often the first to be banished by tyrannical regimes, or excommunicated by the guardians of truth, or censored by the socially comfortable. The poet, as Walter Brueggemann notes, is often the one who cries out in a "public processing of pain." This poetic and

25. Leclercq, *The Love of Learning and the Desire for God*.
26. Rahner, "Poetry and the Christian," 365.
27. Soelle, *The Silent Cry*, 3.
28. Maritain, *Creative Intuition in Art and Poetry*, 74.

prophetic act "releases new social imagination" such that "the cry of pain begins the formation of a counter-community around an alternate perception of reality."[29] Dorothy Day is one example of a prophetic voice whose typewriter and Catholic Worker houses sought to witness to and alleviate the world's pain.[30]

The poetical re-naming and re-imagining of the world is essential to the prophetic task. In the midst of a world too often frozen over with cold indifference, there is still this prayer that asks: "*What if?*—the possible. *What if—?*—the first revolutionary question, the question the dying forces don't know how to ask."[31] Only living forces know how to feel the world with "question-prayers," to envision different futures, to name new possibilities, to believe that something else might be the case than is the case. Perhaps this is why poets and prophets never tire of saying, "I have a dream . . . " or, "the kingdom of God is like . . . "—so that we might transform despair, indifference, anger and isolation into the startling poetical-practical-prophetic-question-prayer: "What if . . . ?"

According to Adrienne Rich, a "revolutionary" poem may do its work in a variety of forms:

> It may do its work in the language and images of dreams, lists, love letters, prison letters, meditations, cries of pain, documentary fragments, blues, late-night long-distance calls . . . Any truly revolutionary art is an alchemy through which waste, greed, brutality, frozen indifference, and anger are transmuted into some drenching recognition of the *What if?*—the possible . . . In depicting lives ordinarily downpressed, shredded, erased, this art reveals through fierce attention their innate and latent vitality and beauty . . .
>
> Revolutionary art dwells, by its nature, on edges: the tension between the *is* and what can be. Edges between ruin and celebration. Naming and mourning damage, keeping pain vocal so it cannot become normalized and acceptable. Yet, through that burning gauze in a poem which flickers over words and images, through the energy of desire, summoning a different reality.[32]

---

29. Brueggemann, *Hope Within History*, 16–20.
30. Day, *The Duty of Delight*.
31. Rich, *What is Found There*, 241–42.
32. Rich, *What is Found There*, 241–42.

PROLOGUE

THE POETRY OF WITNESS

There is a stark question that has haunted poetry (and perhaps all artistic endeavors) in the wake of human atrocities. It is a difficult and interruptive question. What point is poetry in the face of the world's horrors and injustices? Can one be a poet in a world of so much pain? Surely what is called for is concrete action rather than the writing of poetry. Or, is the poetic soul required even more so in the midst of human suffering?

Edmond Jabés, poet of questions and exile, speaks of humanity's struggle to "group letters according to life." He writes in the voice of one of his imaginary rabbis:

> "If we cannot create the vault of heaven," said Reb Josua, "it is because we do not know the mysterious arrangement of letters with which heaven and earth were conceived.
>
> "If we cannot stop the light from going out, it is because the combination of letters that could save it from the dark is unknown to us.
>
> "If we cannot help regarding you, O death, as the absurd and painful toll of our existence, it is because we do not know how to group letters according to life, which would make you its leaven instead of its end.
>
> "If we cannot save you in your last hour, O human being, it is because the secret disposition of letters that would retain your breath escapes us.
>
> "Our books are books of ignorance."
>
> And he added: "Ah, which of these letters that form only one impotent word, witness to our impotence? God disdains them. Yet it is through them that we can read God."[33]

In his haunting work, *The Writing of the Disaster,* Maurice Blanchot says that disaster ruins writing and wrecks language. How do we write in the aftermath of disaster? What words suffice? Is writing possible? What type of writing? There are no words. Yet do we just remain silent? According to Blanchot, silence and blank pages are not the only testimony. He urges us to "keep watch over absent meaning."[34] When we keep watch over absence, we are keeping watch over a vast "text" that is full of questions, cries and desperate yearnings.

---

33. Jabés, *The Book of Resemblances,* 31.
34. Blanchot, *The Writing of the Disaster,* 42.

Prologue

Carolyn Forché introduces her volume, *Against Forgetting: Twentieth Century Poetry of Witness*, with the following story. In 1944, Hungarian poet Miklós Radnóti was sent to a forced-labor camp. He was able to attain a small notebook in which he wrote his last ten poems. When the German soldiers realized they were facing inevitable defeat, they decided to evacuate the camp and, after a long march with the prisoners and with no place to leave them, they executed Radnóti and twenty-one others. However, Forché notes, "the story does not end—as millions of such stories ended—with execution and the anonymity of a mass grave." At the end of the war, Radnóti's wife joined others to exhume a mass grave in the village of Abda. The coroner's report for "corpse #12" read: "A visiting card with the name Dr. Miklós Radnóti printed on it. An ID card stating the mother's name as Ilona Grosz. Father's name illegible. Born in Budapest, May 5, 1909. Cause of death: shot in the nape. In the back pocket of the trousers a small notebook was found soaked in the fluids of the body and blackened by wet earth. This was cleaned and dried in the sun."[35]

Forché cites Radnóti's last notebook entry, dated October 31, 1944:

> I fell beside him; his body turned over,
> already taught as string about to snap.
> Shot in the back of the neck. That's how you too will end,
> I whispered to myself; just lie quietly.
> Patience now flowers into death.
> *Der springt noch auf,* a voice said above me.
> On my ear, blood dried, mixed with filth.[36]

Forché remarks that this verse describes the death of Radnóti's fellow prisoner Miklós Lorsi, a violinist, and is the only trace of his dying. The poem calls out to us from the other side of extremity and is our only evidence that an event has occurred—it exists for us as the trauma of an occurrence.

The poetry of witness is a form of *testimonio*. These poems come to testify, to inscribe, to contest, "but never to leave things as they are."[37] They are a protest against violence and against forgetting, seeking "to redeem

---

35. Forché, *Against Forgetting,* 29.
36. Forché, *Against Forgetting,* 32.
37. Forché, *Against Forgetting,* 32–33.

speech from the silence of pain, and integrity from the disintegrating forces of extremity."[38]

When there is nothing else except a dark night and bleakness, there is still poetry and prayer. Poetry is essential to the human spirit. So essential, that even in humanity's darkest moments, poetry-music-art was created and, in the process, helped humanity survive. Paul Celan, Jewish poet and survivor of the Holocaust, writes of the poetic experience in the following words:

> Reachable, near and not lost, there remained in the midst of the losses this one thing: language . . . In this language I have sought, during those years and the years since then, to write poems: so as to speak, to orient myself, to find out where I was and where I was meant to go, to sketch out reality for myself . . .
>
> A poem, as a manifestation of language and thus essentially dialogue, can be a message in a bottle, sent out in the—not always greatly hopeful—belief that somewhere and sometime it could wash up on land, on heartland perhaps. Poems in this sense are underway: they are making toward something . . . toward an addressable Thou, an addressable realty.[39]

THE WORD BECOME FLESH

While the Christian understanding of divine incarnation is foreign to Jewish spirituality, the idea of God's humility is not. In what sense? Levinas puts it this way: "It is a God whose grandeur, whose justice and *rachamim* (mercy) you see everywhere. It is Christian too, I do not say it is uniquely Jewish. You see his humility; it is a God who comes down . . . who has not negated the finite and who has entered into the finite . . . This means it is a God who has sent you the other human being . . . It is the constitution of society . . . there is a human being sent toward the other human being. That is my central thesis and consequently it is this structure that is divinity."[40]

In the Jewish tradition there is an inseparable bond between God's descent and his elevation. "Terms evoking Divine Majesty and loftiness are often followed or preceded by those describing God bending down to look

---

38. Forché *Against Forgetting*, 45.
39. Celan, *Selected Poems and Prose*, 395–96.
40. Levinas (with Wyschogrod), "Interview with Emmanuel Levinas," 107.

at human misery or *inhabiting* human misery."[41] Levinas cites Psalm 147: "He who heals the broken in heart and binds up their wounds" is also the one "who counts the number of stars and gives them all their names."

When speaking to Christian audiences, Levinas often referred to chapter twenty-five of Matthew's Gospel: "in so far as you did this to one of the least . . ." Of this passage he says: "The relation to God is presented there as a relation to another human person. It is not a metaphor; in the other, there is a real presence of God. In my relation to the other, I hear the word of God. It is not a metaphor. It is not only extremely important; it is literally true. I'm not saying that the other is God, but that in his or her face I hear the word of God."[42]

I am reminded of two sayings from the Rabbinic tradition, brought to my attention in Heschel's masterful study, *Heavenly Torah*.[43] The first saying states that the "Torah is not in heaven" (cf. Deut 30:12). Rather, it is given to us—"on earth"—to wrestle with its teachings and to activate its meanings. The second saying states that the "Torah is a gift from heaven." It communicates or reveals God's intentions for the world and guides us along the path of life; it teaches us how to live "on earth, as it is in heaven."

In Christian language, one might be tempted to say that the incarnate word also expresses or reveals the transcendent word. The finite also "contains" or reveals the infinite. Thus the finite is to be treasured as the honored place where the infinite comes to pass.

The Christian tradition wagers that there is an intimate relationship between human experience—living, suffering, joyous—and the word of God—born, crucified, risen. We always live with the possibility of hearing and responding to "the word become flesh."

Catholic theologian Karl Rahner defends human poetry as essential to the human spirit. "In times when humanism and poetry seem to be dying, buried under the achievements of technological skill and suffocated under the chatter of the masses, Christianity must defend human culture and the poetic word."[44] He draws upon Christianity's incarnational theology to affirm poetry. "The poetic word and the poetic ear are so much part of humanity that if this essential power were really lost to the heart, we could

---

41. Levinas, *In the Time of the Nations*, 101.
42. Levinas, *Is It Righteous to Be?*, 171.
43. Heschel, *Heavenly Torah*, 321–40; 658–79.
44. Rahner, "Poetry and the Christian," 364

no longer hear the word of God in the word of humanity."[45] He bemoans the dry and prosaic theology of boring academics: "Has theology become more perfect because theologians have become prosaic?" Rather, "great poetry exists where humanity radically faces the human condition. The mature Christian will welcome all really great poetry openly and without embarrassment."[46]

Poetic experience signals the very real possibility of hearing the word become flesh. "Ever since this Word has been heard in its human embodiment, there is a brightness and a secret promise in every word."[47] The divine is forever made human—incarnate, translatable—"yours is the flesh we wear."[48] In every authentically human word, the gracious incarnation of God's own word can take place. In the spirituality of Rahner—which is different to but not in opposition to Levinas' "kenosis"—"If one is to grow ever more profoundly Christian [or mature in religious belief], one must never cease to practice listening for this incarnational possibility in the human word."[49]

POETRY'S VITALITY AND PERSONALITY

Poetry attends to the concrete and particular, rather than to speculative schemas and generalizations. As Maritain notes, poetry "is directed toward concrete existence, that is to say, each time toward some singular existent, toward some complex of concrete and individual reality."[50] According to David Tracy, the poet "embarks upon a journey of intensification into the concreteness of each particular reality—*this* body, *this* people, *this* community, *this* tree, *this* place, *this* moment, *this* neighbor—until the very concreteness in any particular reality releases us to sense the concreteness of the whole as internally related through and through."[51]

In attending to concrete existence and singular reality, poetry "makes things diaphanous and alive, and populated with infinite horizons." The poet pays attention to the *livingness of things* that "abound with significance

   45. Rahner, "Poetry and the Christian," 363
   46. Rahner, Poetry and the Christian," 363
   47. Rahner, "Poetry and the Christian," 362.
   48. Cohen, "Avalanche" (adapted).
   49. Rahner, "Poetry and the Christian," 362.
   50. Maritain, *Creative Intuition in Art and Poetry*, 126.
   51. Tracy, *The Analogical Imagination*, 282.

and swarm with meanings."[52] This inherent vitality of life can be expressed by another word— "personality"—a word that is richer in meanings than the rather dull or lifeless word "concrete." Rather, personality evokes the *thou-like* character of living beings.

To speak of life's distinctive personality is difficult. John Macmurray, a Scottish philosopher writing in the nineteen-thirties, raised his voice in the name of personality, yet he always found his task frustrating. "It is a shallow civilization we've got," he wrote in a letter to a friend, "people don't seem to know what I mean when I talk about a *personal* life. 'What's the use of it?' is what they ask."[53] Speaking of the personal life, he writes: "It is amazing how blind we are to this simplest and commonest of all our fields of experience, and to the manner in which it determines and conditions all the others. The last thing we seem to become aware of in our conscious reflection is one another and the concrete ties that bind us together in the bundle of life."[54]

To think about personality—to write and speak of it—is difficult because personality doesn't like to be called an "it" at all. Personality is not a concept, something that can be conceptualized or pinned-down (or even less, something that can be utilized), because personality refuses to be treated as a "thing."[55] Nevertheless, Erazim Kohák attempts a definition of sorts, saying that personality "is the decision to treat the Person, the Person-al mode of being, as the ultimate metaphysical category."[56] Personality means that things are vital and alive, rather than subsumed into anonymous and impersonal structures.

According to Russian religious philosopher Nikolai Berdyaev, most of us live somewhat unthinkingly in the context of social arrangements and cultural norms that shape the way we live in the world. Yet personality is the exception to all of this: "In human personality there is much that is generic, belonging to the human race, much which belongs to history, tradition, society, class, family . . . much that is 'common.' But it is precisely this which is not 'personal' in personality. That which is personal is original . . . Personality is the exception, not the rule. The secret of the existence of

---

52. Maritain, *Creative Intuition in Art and Poetry,* 127.
53. Macmurray, *Reason and Emotion,* xi.
54. Macmurray, *Reason and Emotion,* 153.
55. Veling, "The Personal and Spiritual Life."
56. Kohak, *The Embers and the Stars,* 126.

personality lies in its absolute irreplaceability, its happening but once, its uniqueness, its incomparableness."[57]

"Personality is the exception, not the rule." Personality asks us to think exceptionally rather than routinely. Personality requires an almost saintly attention to the often unnoticed—the singular one amidst the crowd. There may well be a hundred, but there is also the one. Personality represents a great difficulty for anyone who seeks all-encompassing theories or all-embracing standards. Personality is not made to measure or made to fit. Rather, it is immeasurable and cannot be contained.

Martin Buber notes that personality also finds expression in the natural world. "I contemplate a tree," he writes. In doing so, "I can assign it to a species"; "I can overcome its uniqueness"; "I can dissolve it into a number." In all these ways, "the tree remains my object and has its place." However, Buber continues, "it can also happen, if will and grace are joined, that as I contemplate the tree, I am drawn into a relation, and the tree ceases to be an *It*. The power of exclusiveness has seized me."[58] Personality is concerned with all that addresses and reveals itself to me in its *thou-like* originality.

It seems appropriate that the first book of the Bible is called *Genesis* or *Bereshit*. In the beginning God did not create religion—God created the world, which means that God created plants and animals and the starry sky and you and me. This is God's primary revelation, not religion. If religion means anything, then it means I am caught up in this bundle of life and that my existence is not solitary; rather it is relationally implicated. Religion is a matter of living relations between us. Divine and human love are interlaced and invested with each other, rather than alienated in separate and disconnected realms. The duty of religious faith is to humanize our world or to "personalize" our world, to overcome the world of *It* and welcome the presence of *Thou*. This is also what it means to divinize our world—hallowing each other and each created life as sacred and holy.

Attention to the beauty and singularity of personality magnifies, rather than diminishes, our apprehension of the Divine. There is a holy spark in every living creature and every human being. Can we say that the ocean has personality? I'm sure a seafarer would say so—not only of the ocean, but of the wind as well. The geologist and the sculptor know the personality of granite and marble. The farmer and the gardener know the personality of soil and plants. The conservationist knows the personality of rainforests

---

57. Berdyaev, *Slavery and Freedom*, 23–24.
58. Buber, *I and Thou*, 57–58.

and wetlands. Indigenous people have long taught us that there is spirit and personality in all living creatures—in earth and sky, in land and ocean, in the natural ecologies of life that sustain us all.

If we could let go of our arrogance, perhaps we could see that there is friendship in creation. Think of birds, for example. They are perhaps one of our shiest creatures, born of the air and distant to us, which is why I especially love it when they draw close and display amazing trust across the barrier of our strangeness, as though there were some primal part of them that recognized creation's friendship. I love this capacity for friendship expressed in the wild and the untamed. Communion in creation is a wonderful gift—if only we could listen and be attentive, if only we could believe that there are, as poets remind us, "real presences" in life, real signs of vitality and personality.[59]

DIVINE LOVE

Poets open themselves to divine presence whilst knowing that God is not a thing or an object to be spoken of. The relation to God is more akin to desire than to knowledge. God rarely comes to us propositionally or purely rationally. Commenting on his translation of Martin Buber's *I and Thou*, Walter Kaufmann writes: "God cannot be spoken of, but God can be spoken to. God cannot be seen, but God can be listened to. The only possible relation with God is to address him and to be addressed by him, here and now."[60] For most people of faith, God is not a theory or a problem, a treatise or a dogma, a speculation or a doctrine, a *this* or a *that*. God is the one who hears our prayers, more than the one we talk about. It is more important to speak to God rather than about God. "Go into your room and shut the door and pray to your Father who is in secret" (Matt 6:6). For most people, God is their deepest and secret hope, the one they talk to, the one they pray to, the one who listens and understands. In speech, as also in prayer, "we do not just think of the interlocutor, we speak to him."[61]

Amidst the hardships of life, God is the miraculous one. God can do what seems impossible, can change what seems hopeless, can soften even the hardest heart. For the poetic soul, God is personal, relational, mysterious, and intimate.

59. Steiner, *Real Presences*.
60. Kaufmann, "I and You," 26.
61. Levinas, *Entre Nous*, 32.

"To sense the sacred," Abraham Heschel says, "is to sense what is dear to God."[62] The concerns of God are personal. If not, then I don't know how we can speak of God's relationality, or God's communication, or God's justice and mercy. These concerns are either matters of personal concern or empty "matter-less" theories. It is difficult for systems and constructs to capture these concerns because much of our systematic and abstract thought is empty of personality. Personality can only be experienced in relational encounter, yet most of our lives are distracted by the structures and routines of impersonal existence. It takes a poetic soul and a responsive awareness to embrace God's personal concerns.

The concerns of God are personal. They are the concerns of dignity—the dignity of each human person and every living being—not as pieces in a system or players in a grand scheme—but as personal, living entities—unique and irreplaceable. God's personal love means that people of different creeds, people of different nationalities, people of different social and economic backgrounds—can share friendship. It is not that the differences between us do not matter; indeed, they are often the basis for the infinite variety of relationships that can be shared in our interpersonal lives. Yet when we cling to our differences or guard them in fear, we lose sight of God's love and are living instead in a world of labels and name-calling: you are this, you are that; they are this, they are that. Love helps us to find joy in living together, to seek mutual understanding, to share experience, to express and reveal ourselves to one another. This is all that is required of us—to put down our swords, surrender our defenses, and share in the spirit of friendship which is the essence of the personal, poetic and spiritual life.

---

62. Heschel, *Who is Man?*, 49.

1

In the Beginning

CATALOGUING

> And out of the ground the Lord God formed every animal of the field and every bird of the air, and brought them to Adam to see what he would call them; and whatsoever Adam called every living being, that was the name thereof. —Genesis 2:19

It is a natural instinct for human beings to catalogue and to order, to group things and to name things. Think of the Periodic Table or the Dewey Decimal System, for example.

Recently, while living on the land, I became interested in bird life, plant life and star life. I learnt that each of these natural entities have their own specific catalogues or naming structures. The stars, for example, are catalogued according to the "NGC," which stands for the *New General Catalogue,* originally devised in 1888, to list and describe the then known 8000 deep sky objects.[1] It seems that humans have been audacious enough to map and order even the vast night sky of the universe.

In the early part of the twentieth century, our galaxy was thought to be the entire universe. What we now know as distant galaxies were then thought to be whirlpools of gas in *our* galaxy (hence they were called *nebulae,* a term we still use today). It wasn't until the 1940s that astronomers realized that

---

1. Thompson, *The Australian Guide to Stargazing,* 12.

these whirlpool-like nebulae were actually galaxies themselves. This singular discovery instantaneously made our universe billions of times larger.[2]

It seems there are no bounds to what humans seek to catalogue and name. Even the ephemeral clouds are catalogued. I recall a cloud chart on my balcony that displayed various types of clouds and their particular designations, for example, cumulus, cirrus, stratus, etc. I also remember watching a documentary about a soil microbiologist who was able to see whole microscopic "universes" happening within one centimeter of topsoil.

Naming and cataloguing are ways that humans come to understand the natural world around them. They work best in the "sciences," aiding us to better understand the complex structures of life around us.

"Naming the world," however, need not be seen as an exercise of "mastering the world." Rather, as we "give the names" we learn more about the entities revealing themselves to us. Discovering and naming the complex life forms of the natural world aids us in better understanding that world. It is a way of helping us receive the revelation of the natural world.

Cataloguing has certainly helped me, for example, as I have learnt more about plants. I have even come to respect some of the Latin names such as *lomandra longifolia,* which I would never have known except that I was advised to choose this plant for growing on clay soils around the banks of our dam, to aid filtration from run-off and the dam's water quality.

Similarly, I regularly refer to my copy of the *Field Guide to Australian Birds.* I now have a list of some dozen birds that visit the aforementioned dam, and I am able to recognize honeyeaters, finches and fantails. Being able to name and identify these shy creatures aids me in appreciating their beauty and wonder. They are no longer "just birds." Rather, I am able to notice a "red-browed finch" or a "grey fantail" or a "scarlet honeyeater," as they dart in and out of the branches in front of me.

Australian indigenous people have long had their own unique way of naming the natural world around them. They may not have used "scientific categories," yet they "mapped" their intimate knowledge of the natural world in stories or "song-lines," rather than in the "cataloguing" way of scientific description. It seems there is something primal or elemental in the Genesis verse that says, "Adam called every living being."

When it comes to human communities, however, I feel that cataloguing is a dangerous thing. I have never liked words such as "race" or "class" or "black" or "white" or "left" or "right." Human beings defy categorization.

---

2. Thompson, *The Australian Guide to Stargazing,* 99.

Each person is unique, but then, so too is each and every fantail, and so too is the planet earth.

Recently, I found myself engaging in another form of cataloguing. Over time I have written and collected poetry in spiral-bound notepads. I decided to catalogue these poems. My system was fairly basic. I purchased a small, portable, expanding file-case with alphabetical sleeves. I then went through my dozens of spiral notepads, tore out poems, and filed them according to themes.

It was a more difficult exercise than I initially thought. For a start, many poems seem to encompass more than one theme. Moreover, how does one go about cataloguing poetry that spans a range of different scenarios and emotions over two or more decades? Would it be possible, for example, that a poem I wrote twelve years ago could be catalogued under the same theme as a poem I wrote last week?

I nevertheless decided to try this exercise. I found myself tearing up my notepads and cataloguing pages of torn-out poems under different themes. I ended up with seven sleeves in my portable expanding file into which I filed my poems, under the following categories:

1. In the Beginning
2. Resistance
3. Time, Death, Memory
4. Singularity
5. Natural Lover
6. Desire
7. You/Divinity

Don't ask me how or why these seven themes emerged. Yet somehow, as I went through my spiral-bound notepads and tore out poems to file, these were the divisions into which they fell.

In the process, I felt like I was learning something about the "themes" of my own life emerging from decades of spiral-bound poetry, torn-out, filed, and catalogued.

TWENTY-SIX LETTERS

Imagine yourself sitting alone in a library. It is deadly quiet and there is no one else around. Just you and the endless corridors of shelved books—their physical presence, their vast array, their stubborn existence, their refusal to die—an almost haunting presence of souls embalmed in words.

They exist in solidarity with one another—back to back, standing upright and tall, with emblazoned spines—some long forgotten, yet waiting nevertheless, almost obstinately, for that day when a hand will reach up and once again bring its pages to life.

Amidst all these books—stretching across centuries and centuries, filled with voices of seemingly endless wisdom and reflection, engaging in innumerable disciplines—amidst all these books you suddenly realize that you are in the presence of, and surrounded by, twenty-six letters.

Twenty-six letters—no more or no less—all of them arranged and re-arranged in a seemingly infinite myriad of ways. And even now as I write, I too am simply another who is arranging and combining twenty-six letters.

NAKED

I rarely share my poetry and I wonder why? Maybe because it is too intimate or personal? No, I don't fear expressing myself. I think all human beings have an innate desire to express and reveal themselves, to note that this life means something, says something, counts for something. To create is our dignity. It is the reason we were born.

I don't fear the intimacy of poetry. Indeed, this is why I read and love poetry, because I feel I am encountering deeply real and personal worlds.

So why? Why do I fear sharing poetry?

When I was ten years old, I had no such fear. I wrote my ten-year-old poems and sent them to the editor of the Children's Pages in the local newspaper. And then, with wondrous expectancy, I would wait, child-eyed, until the weekly edition finally appeared—and there was *my poem*—printed—my voice, my words, my expression. I would look in wonder at the amazing beauty of words, embodying my young thoughts and expressing my personal world.

So why do I fear sharing poetry?

Is it because I am older now, and no longer youthful and exuberant or naïve and trusting, but rather shriveled by fear—by judgement and correction, assessment and adjudication, approval and non-approval?

What scares me so? Why am I fearful?

And so, I take on a mask—a cover and a rationale—knowing that I can never ever really expose myself.

At Last

The next one is going to be real
Finally
After years in academia
Finally
I'm going to do something real.

Talmudic Creativity

"I gave you flax
and you created a garment
I gave you wheat
and you baked bread."

Raw Materials

How many colours are there
on the artist's palette?

How many letters are there
in the English alphabet?

Old Technology

How beautiful it must have been
to write poetry
with the feather of a bird.

Let Go

Everything within me is saying
Let go

Yet there are so many things
I cling to
so many things
holding me back

I cannot let go of everything
There are some things
that won't let me go
that bind me fast and
hold me tight

Other things feel like
dead weight
like stuff I've been
dragging around
for years and years

How do I let this go?
the immoveable
the lifeless
the useless weight

How to find again
amidst the weariness and
restlessness

the light burden
the easy yoke.

"Rave On" (VM)

Speak what you feel
Say what you mean
Say it all
No matter what
Rave on
Like Jesus
Like Jabès
Like the wind.

Hot Off the Press

When you write
it should always be hot off the press

Now's your chance
write whatever you will

No one's looking
write whatever you dare

Say it all
Say it now
as though this is what you meant to say.

I'm Not Dead Yet

I'm not going to disappear
   I'm going to re-emerge.

Put Pen to Paper

Why?
Because it is the only real chance I have
to say what I think and what I feel.

Poetry

Poetry is prose
freed of regulation.

Cut Loose

Don't keep it secreted away
in hidden journals

Or tucked away
in old notebooks

It's time to let it go
It's time to release

It's time to say
what you always wanted to say.

Vocation

You are better at what you want to do
when you do what you are meant to do.

Exposure

No hiding place
no pretense
no cleverness.

The Curative Way

The only way I can write like this
is out of a certain
dis-ease
Yet confident nevertheless
in the curative way.

A Page a Day

You turn a page
each day of your life

This is the way life is read

You inscribe a page
each day of your life

This is the way life is written.

Source

Work with
your own
material.

A New Page

Every poem
deserves a new page.

The Crumpled Page

The crumpled page on the floor
the poem rejected
nonetheless plays its part
in those better poems
accepted.

Limited Region

I do not always write about things I know

Sometimes writing takes me far beyond
this limited region.

Let Time Do Its Work

There are so many hours of non-writing
contained in the few hours
of writing.

Editing

Editing is like fine-tuning
an instrument.

Deleting

Deleting means choosing what is worth keeping which makes deleting an essential and difficult task.

Aphorism

How do you write an aphorism?
You keep cutting it back and back
until very little remains
except the essential

How do you live an aphoristic life?

Clean Paper

You have clean paper
curse of blankness
or promise of newness

You can always put your mark
on things
You can always begin
again

You have clean paper
pure
white
unadulterated

You can always write words
on new pages
You can always turn blankness
into blessing.

Gliding

My gliding pilot told me
that the worst thing you can do is stall

The best way to pick up speed
is to point your nose downwards and dive

Sometimes going down is the best way to get lift
to let airflow over your wings

So that you can keep soaring
above it all.

2

Resistance

FAULT LINES

The poetic thinker will never find a secure home in the Academy that, sadly and disturbingly, has become ensnared in rankings, metrics and bureaucratic corporatization. If you are looking for the poetic thinker, do not first look to the Academy. They are not there. They are Dorothy Day's typewriter and Catholic Worker houses. They are Jean Vanier's L'Arche communities. They are Paulo Friere's peasants learning to read. They are Gustavo Guitérrez's poor. They are Martin Luther King's freedom riders.

They are the ones tracking the fault lines, cracks and fissures in a system that is always breaking.

After the birth of his daughter, Brazilian poet-theologian, Rubem Alves, spoke of his own disenchantment with academia: "I broke with the academic style because I decided that life was very short, very mysterious, and I didn't have time to waste with academics. I would only say things in the most honest manner. If people like it, fine. If not, I can't help that. Today I couldn't write academically even if I wanted to."[1] He lamented the fact that within academic circles, the great questions and mysteries of life became little more than clever "trapezes" where "intellectual virtuosities" were performed. Alves broke free from a world of academia that he perceived as hollow, pretentious and lacking real relevance. Academia—especially in the humanities—had lost its flesh and become little more than dry bones.

1. Keefe-Perry, *Way to Water*, 43 (citing an interview with Alves).

I confess that the world of "academic freedom" no longer feels like a world of freedom to me. While I understand that many human endeavors are bound by certain prescriptions, I have always been attracted to the idea that places of learning should enjoy some freedom or non-attachment to convention or standards. The virtue of academic freedom exists not for itself, but in order to allow for the discovery, invention or expression of new thought. When the academy begins to feel like a prison, it is inevitable that the free spirit of inquiry will escape, leaving the bars behind for the open fields of wonder and discovery.

THE MYSTERY OF TEARS

In the Australian Broadcasting Commission podcast series titled, "Imagine This," young children raise intriguing questions and receive responses from adults who try to answer them.

The question for this particular episode comes from a young girl named Grace. "Why do tears come out of our eyes when we cry?"

The host of the program, Brianna, praises Grace for asking such a wonderful and poignant question. She notes that tears are something we all have in common. Every human being cries from the moment we are born.

"Where do you think tears come from?" Brianna asks the child. "From our eyes," Grace says, and then she adds, "When you cry, it is from your heart, because our hearts can break easily."

"How do these tears get all the way from our heart to our eyes?" Brianna asks. "They go through our body," Grace replies.

Brianna continues the dialogue. "Yes, the tears come out of our eyes, and our eyes are part of our body, so our body must make them from somewhere, but where do they actually come from? Is there a bucket of tears hiding in our body?"

"I don't know," Grace says.

"This sounds like a mystery," Brianna says, "and I think the person we should ask to help us solve this mystery is Michelle, a Senior Lecturer in Anatomy, which means she teaches people what the body is made of."

"Can you give us a lesson in tears today?" Brianna asks Michelle. "We are trying to find out where the tears come from."

Michelle responds quite confidently. "Our body has tiny little factories called glands."

"What are glands?" Grace asks. Michelle explains. "Glands can make us sweat. Glands can make our mouth water. And glands can make tears."

"Okay," Brianna says, "but let's focus on the eye glands. What are tears?"

Grace is quick to respond, "Water!" "And salt!"

"Right," says Michelle. "And we always have a little bit of these salty tears in our eyes to help keep them clean, to wash out dust, for example."

"But what about the other kind of tears, the ones that feel like they come from our heart?" Brianna asks.

Michelle responds, "If we are really happy or really sad, or when we can't get our own way, we cry."

"But why does our body make *those* tears happen?" Brianna asks.

"That's still a big mystery," Michelle responds. "There are some things that even scientists don't know."

"Do animals cry?" Brianna asks.

"Not when they are happy or sad. Animals cry when something gets caught in their eye. They can make tears. But they don't cry the same way as us."

"Do boys cry, like girls?"

"For sure they cry."

"Do Mums cry?"

"Yes, Mums cry."

"Do Dads cry?"

"They probably won't tell you, but they do cry."

"Does every single person on this planet cry?"

"Yes, that's what makes us human."

Brianna offers this summation to Grace's question: "So Grace, these special glands help us make tears in our body to wash away dirt and keep our eyes healthy and clean. But the reason we cry tears that feel like they come from our heart—well, that's one of the mysteries of being human. We don't quite know yet."

Divinity

"I will bleach your sins
and I will note your goodness"
says the Lord.

Suffering

There are many forms of suffering
many types and degrees
yet the commonest of all
is the suffering we share.

Recluse

You haven't gone out lately?
No, I've been caught
trapped
bound
tied
constrained
confined
caged
roped
hung
sunk
shipwrecked.

To Do

You did what you wanted to do
You got away
You went looking for peace

It wasn't a question of
Should I or Shouldn't I?
You simply did what you wanted to do

This is almost a miracle
For it is virtually impossible
To do what you want to do.

Without Peace

We do not live very easily or comfortably
No one escapes the disturbance of being
It is not for peace that we were made.

I Carry the Death of Christ in My Body

I carry the death of Christ in my body
I feel it in the pit of my stomach
I sense it in the tension of my muscles
I know it in the anguish of my mind
I carry the death of Christ in my body.

Monastery

Pray for those who can pray no more
Pray as though
only your prayers were left.

Job

Why does Job presume it was God who afflicted him
Why does he not take task with the devil?

Perhaps because he knows (is instructed)
that the Lord our God, the Lord is One.

"Everybody Knows" (LC)

When you realize the world is screwed
you are less likely to spend your energies
pointing that fact out to everyone.

Justice

Justice: It's not fair!
Injustice: Why am I being hurt?

Lament

He believed in God
yet it caused him such sorrow

What reason could there be
to believe in God?

It caused him great confusion
it caused him great pain

Why believe in God
why suffer so much?

Gethsemane

That night in the garden
under a full moon
on the hills of Jerusalem
among the olive trees
when everyone had gone to sleep
you sweated blood
and poured yourself out
to save your Father's Name
lifting yourself higher and higher
into the Kingdom of Heaven.

Seek First the Kingdom of Heaven

Empty what you want
down to what you need

Take your desire
strip it bare
down to the essential

Cut yourself
to the right measure

Seek first
the largeness of God's kingdom

Everything else will be given to you
anyway.

Nietzsche

I wish I could say
no regrets
no apologies
no excuses

I wish I could stand up
tall and true
to myself
to my convictions

I wish I could fuck them all
and never have to feel
this dull and deadening
powerlessness.

There Is . . .

Every time I look at the stars
Every time I catch the bus from work
Every time I talk with her
Every time I read or write

No rest, no escape, no rescue

Every time
In every breath
In every moment
Always, always.

Anxiety

I've seen it all go down
in the blink of an eye

No rhyme or reason
just the blink of an eye

Things are out of my hands
I have no control

Everything changes
in the blink of an eye

What can I trust
or what can I love?

When everything happens
in the blink of an eye.

Venom

Poison
Deadly
It will kill you
Maybe not straight away
like a gunshot to the head
yet it will slowly work its way through you

Once it enters your bloodstream
it goes straight to your heart
paralyzing
convulsing
killing you

What you need is a tourniquet
and as quickly as possible
you need an antidote.

Temptation

Get thee behind me
all you churches
all you choruses
all you tempters
all you singers of praises

I am not there
I have gone to a place
you do not know.

"Wipe the Dust Off Your Feet"

We can't be too sentimental
We also have to be able to say
Piss off

Even Jesus said
Get thee behind me
Which in my language means

Piss off
Go away
Leave me alone.

Social Construction

You can't let them make you
into something you're not

Don't let them take your spirit

Stay true
like an arrow.

The Boss

The big man arrives
9.00am on Monday morning

He passes each office
and moves in a way that says
"I have arrived"

He calls a meeting
sets the agenda
and conducts everyone's affairs

The big man arrives
9.00am on Monday morning

And yet
hardly anyone cares.

Leadership

The person who makes everyone feel small
or the person of Great Size.

Truth and Lies

As much as things can be a lie
false and illusory
so too things can be a truth
clear and certain

There are lies
and there are truths
and both are dangerous.

Believing in God

"Do you believe in God?"

Only when there is war and hatred
    when it is utterly necessary.

Thy Kingdom Come

If it is thy kingdom
where is your realm?

If you are master of the universe
why don't you rule?

If your will be done
why do you need me?

"Divinity Keeps Its Distances" (EL)

God does not too quickly
join ranks
with human affairs.

Current Affairs

Wouldn't a better description be
Endless Affairs.

"Love your..."

It is not too difficult to know why
we do injury to our enemies

What is more difficult is to wonder why
we injure those closest to us.

Christ Descended into Hell

> It is not glory at first
> but hell.

Mercy

Do not be duped by those who say
it is just a matter of being kind and loving people

Fools!

Don't they know their own hearts?
Don't they know their own hypocrisy?

All we have in the end
is no beautiful or romantic message of love

All we have
is our broken heart, our broken love, our broken ideal
and our quest for mercy.

No Agenda

Give me a
"no agenda" person
any day.

Positivity

Don't align yourself
with negativity
no matter how tempting

Always align yourself
with positivity
no matter how futile.

Where are the Saints?

Where are the large hearts
the people of size?

Where are the saints
crazy with love?

They are the crushed ones
at the bottom of the pack

Bearing the weight
of narrow-minded people.

Powers and Principalities

There are many powers that operate in life

There are the powers of state
the court, the president, the judge

There are the powers of business
the bank, the boardroom, the lender

There are the powers of nations
determining the fate
of vast human populations

There are many powers that operate in life
They are multifarious and manifold
like a seven-headed beast

But then there is you
who comes to me un-powerfully
who sleeps next to me, side-by-side

You who casts their lot with me
and doesn't care anymore
except that we have been welded like steel.

Two Games

There are two games to choose from
one has no rhyme or reason
the other is absolutely required.

3

Time, Death, Memory

BEN A. J. VELING (1929-2013)

I remember being with my father in the palliative care ward. I remember being locked in a gaze of compassion—inexpressible really—looking into his eyes and feeling an enormous love. "It's okay Dad. I love you and you are loved."

    At the conclusion of my father's funeral, a thin gossamer veil was drawn across his coffin like a final curtain. Gossamer is silky and satin—like a bower-bird—dark in the shadows and glinting in the sunlight. See-through yet disappearing. A brief moment where life and death touch. It only lasts a while. The dead do not stay very long, just long enough to say goodbye, and then they're gone, waiting for us on the far side.

PAUL RICOEUR (1913-2005)

"Where are our dead?" asks Paul Ricoeur. Even secular societies ask this question. Religious or non-religious, we do not treat our dead as "trash," like putting out the garbage. We honor our dead and ritualize their memory. Nevertheless, Ricoeur wonders, is this simply "make believe"—a need to preserve the dead in a magical after-life, however conceived?[1]

---

1. Ricoeur, *Living Up To Death*, 8, 16.

As I sat on the bed with my father in the palliative care ward, I knew he was dying, yet I didn't see him as "all but dead," but as still alive—still living—all the way "up to death," as Ricoeur says.

Living up to Death is the title of Ricoeur's last book. Along with an essay he wrote when his wife was ill and dying ("Mourning and Cheerfulness"), it contains scribblings from the notepad Ricoeur kept by his bedside as he was dying, including his last written piece of writing titled, "Resurrection" (the book has facsimile copies of his own handwriting). It is a very intimate book, offering the last thoughts of a dying man who devoted his life to philosophical and theological inquiry.

In the essay on his wife's approaching death, Ricoeur reflects on the palliative care nurses who didn't see her as "all-but-dead," but who saw her as "alive and living" right up to the point of death. He suggests that, unlike Martin Heidegger who said we were "beings-unto-death," the palliative care nurses mobilized "the deepest resources of life to still affirm life." He admires this insight: "Dying persons do not see themselves as dying, as soon to be dead, but as still living, even up to half an hour before their dying."[2]

"Already dead" is no reason for philosophy. It is life and living—all the way "up to death"—this is the reason.

EMMANUEL LEVINAS (1906–1995)

In an interview titled, "The Philosopher and Death," Levinas notes that only the living ask about death, and yet the living know nothing of it. "That it will come, yes." And yet, death is "what we cannot take upon ourselves." Unlike other things in life, death is not a "project" that we accomplish. "You go toward death, you 'learn to die', you 'prepare' for the last extremity; but there is the last quarter of an hour (or the last second), and at that point it is death that completes the last leg of the journey by itself, and it is a surprise."[3]

There is another aspect of death that is important to Levinas: the death of the other. While we are alive, it is primarily the death of the other that we encounter. Levinas is a survivor of the Nazi horror. He writes: "For the survivor, there is in the death of the other his or her disappearance, and the extreme loneliness of that disappearance. I think *the Human* consists precisely in opening oneself to the death of the other."[4]

---

2. Ricoeur, *Living Up To Death*, 13–14.
3. Levinas, *Alterity and Transcendence*, 8.
4. Levinas, *Alterity and Transcendence*, 157–58.

If we speak of an "after life," this is something we can never know while we are still living. The transcendence of an "after life," however, suggests that there is "a manner of thinking that goes beyond my death." For Levinas, this manner of thinking is encountered in the death of the other person: "Before the death of the other, my neighbor, death the mysterious appears to me as the bringing about of an aloneness toward which I cannot be indifferent. It awakens me to the other."[5] The mortality of my neighbor asks that I not be indifferent to their suffering.

Death does not give us the possibility "to be or not to be." However, what death can never take away is the possibility "to love or not to love."

DOROTHEE SOELLE (1929–2003)

One of Dorothee Soelle's major works is titled, *The Silent Cry: Mysticism and Resistance.* Of the various mystical paths she explores in this book, the one she never addresses is "death." And so in her last book, *The Mystery of Death,* written while she was dying, she decides to include death in "the silent cry."

Soelle battles mightily with the notion of "a continual individual existence."[6] For much of her life she protested the distorted individualism of Western society. Salvation must surely mean more than just saving oneself.

She appreciates Levinas' insight that "the first death is the death of the other."[7] The gospel saying, "he saved others; himself he could not save" (Matt 27:42) suggests that Christ lived for others but had no "power" to save himself.

Soelle wants to affirm death as a natural part of life, yet she also reflects on St. Paul's notion that "the wages of sin is death" (Rom 6:23). There is something that is not good about death. When I heard news from the palliative care ward that my father had died in the small hours of the night, my eyes filled with tears and I blurted out, "Why do people have to die? Death is so cruel, so unnecessary."

Soelle notes that her religious tradition states very clearly: "We are exiled. Our home is heaven. We were driven out of Paradise; what is here cannot possibly be all that is."[8] She goes on to say that this is not a denial

---

5. Levinas, *Alterity and Transcendence,* 161.
6. Soelle, *The Mystery of Death,* 117.
7. Soelle, *The Mystery of Death,* 30.
8. Soelle, *The Mystery of Death,* 73.

of life, but a reminder that the dream of God's kingdom is still important and a "swaggering pragmatism" will not save us. When St. Paul speaks of the "wages of sin," he is speaking of the death that comes into the world through poverty, war and hatred. The greatest enemy is not "natural" death, but the death of my neighbor that comes through violence and oppression: "the creeping death that we see every day in the faces of so many people in our society. This kind of being-without-life, this kind of dying and this kind of death—deserves the utmost resistance, deserves passionate struggle."[9]

Soelle wants to die on the side of life. She cites the medieval hymn: *Ubi caritas et amor, ibi deus est*"—where love is, there is God.[10] The final prose words in her book are:

> "Is everything over when we die?" Only those whose ego is imprisoned within the limits of individual existence . . . can ask this question. "Is everything over when we die" is a godless question . . . No, everything is not over. Everything continues. Everything I lived for, everything I tried to do with other people, everything I started and everything I failed—it all goes on . . . I will no longer breathe as this individual, this woman of the twentieth century, but the air I breathe will be there, for everyone.[11]

JOHNNY CASH (1932-2003)

This is an album that really touched me, *American V: A Hundred Highways* by Johnny Cash. It is his last vocal recordings before he died. The musical arrangements were produced about a year later by his close friend, Rick Rubin.

On the cover notes, Rubin tells the story that just before Johnny died, he noticed how his voice on the other end of the phone was sometimes "weak and almost gasping for air," and other times his voice "boomed with gravity and power." He says that the songs on this album reflect this dying man's last testimony. I certainly felt this as I listened to the song, "God's Gonna Cut You Down," exemplary of Cash's booming, prophetic voice, whereas on the song, "If You Could Read My Mind," his voice is struggling and faltering.

9. Soelle, *The Mystery of Death*, 126.
10. Soelle, *The Mystery of Death*, 105.
11. Soelle, *The Mystery of Death*, 130.

This album represents the last breath of a dying man. It is an intimate encounter. It is also a tribute to the passion of a man who knew suffering and yet was one of the great songwriters of redemption. Imagine him singing to June—the woman who saved his soul—the woman he is grieving over so deeply:

> I pray that God will give me courage
> To carry on 'til we meet again
> It's hard to know she's gone forever
> They're carrying her home on the evening train.[12]

Rubin also tells this story on the cover notes. During one of Johnny's many hospital stays, he heard about an evangelist who was dying of cancer and who took communion every day and claimed that this saved him. Johnny thought there might be something in this, so he asked Rubin if he would share communion with him every day. Rubin agreed, though often the only way they could do this was by phone. Rubin writes: "I had never taken communion before, but Johnny found his old communion kit. He hadn't used it in many years, but Johnny gave me my first communion. We spoke about doing it everyday, and that's how the ritual began. Each day we would speak on the phone and Johnny would perform the communion rite. We would both visualize and internalize, eyes closed. It was performed as a meditation. A moment to connect deeply to the spirit."

Rubin notes that every call ended in the same way:

> I love you John.
> I love you Rick.

There is much in this story for all of us—still living—to learn.

---

12. Johnny Cash, "On the Evening Train," *American V.*

Essential Time

It is good to watch over time
to notice its passing
and the time that remains

It is good to realize that time
is of the essence
that your life drips through
drop by drop
to the very last.

Time Shared

Into time I came
though I do not remember this

From time I shall leave
though I do not know in what way

My comings and goings
are a mystery to me

I only have this time
to which you and I belong

Time is not mine to possess
Time is what I spend with you

All that is alive
shares time with me.

Time Past

I no longer need to search
as much as I once did

Back then
it was as if everything propelled me forward

Whole years were as tomorrow

Whereas now
a few days suffice

It's not that I no longer look forward
Rather, the past assumes more and more weight

75% of my life is already downloaded.

Go Back

I'm too old to worry
whether I'm approved or non-approved

I'm too old to live as though
everything depends on another's stamp

Too old to worry
Too old to please
Too old to succeed

Go back
Go back to those days when nothing seemed insurmountable
Go back to those days when everything seemed possible
Go back to those days when the future
was your wondrous dream.

Wiseman's Ferry

Who was that woman
now coming into memory
standing on the ferry
going nowhere really
just being together
crossing the river
listening to the tambourine man
all the way to St. Albans

Who was that woman?

Memory

The young seek and look forward
The old relinquish and remember

Strange paradox

Our lives reach into the future
only to be drawn back into memory.

Old Age

The time back then
and the time now
do not seem very different.

Revisitation

It happened on a beautiful sunny day
down by the banks of the river
cups of coffee with my mother
86 years of age
watching the old Wiseman's Ferry
chugging back and forth
and remembering a time
back in my youth
when this same scene
was filled with the beauty
of young love.

Skull

When I rest my hands against my cheeks
I can feel the bones of my skull
Death is just millimeters away.

Naked

Death is a teacher
It fills your life like a deep well
It makes your eyes swollen with grief and gratitude

Naked you came into the world
Naked you shall leave
Naked you may as well live.

Dot-Point

I am this dot-point
dot-point of birth
dot-point of death
coming into the world as a beginning
and leaving the world as an end
Dot-point.

Strange Solace

There is solace in the warning
"Do not blow your own trumpet"

There is solace in the starkness
"Death is your lot"

There is solace in the indictment
"No one is just"

There is solace in the finality
"None are spared."

Ethical Time

Imagine time as an ethical requirement
rather than as something
that simply ticks by.

Rest in Peace

I sleep but my heart is awake
I sleep but the dog barks
I sleep but daylight encroaches
I sleep but I find no peace

Is death the ultimate sleep
where nothing awakens and nothing disturbs?

Death is no "rest in peace"
as though all our life simply sought a peace without disturbance

I sleep but my heart is awake
This remains true of the living and the dead.

The End

This is all I've got to go on

"You mean, death?"

"No, I mean God."

Incessant

You are incessant

The stars shine. The ocean heaves. The trees change. The rivers tumble
but I will die

My father will die, my lover, my neighbour, my child
but you are incessant

You refuse to die
You don't give in
You escape while life is dying all around you

And we take comfort in this?
Your incessant being?
Your eternal return, again and again?

You who refuses to die
You who remains
while all around you
life passes away.

The Body Departs

A time will come when the flesh
must let go of time
when the flesh must say to time
as if in a last farewell

"Thank you, you have given me life
Thank you, you have kept me going all the way through
but now I must say goodbye
now I must leave your pulsating seconds
your rushing blood
your entry into my body"

And the body departs
and the time of life and death departs
and those still remaining witness the last goodbye.

Surrender

Many people think of surrender as
giving in or giving up
as though this were an easy thing to do

Yet surrender is one of our most difficult acts
requiring years and years of practice

I know one thing for sure
one thing only
Surrender

"Do not be anxious"

Surrender doesn't mean giving up
It means letting go

of fear, hatred, jealousy, anger, pride,
competition, anxiety, worry . . .

Jabès

It took him a long time
to write

What took him so long?

Was it that he finally realised
after so many failed attempts
that he could only write of this lack?

So that all the while
his striving counted for little

led him at last
to the point

where all he could do was comment
on this struggle with words

And so he names his book
"The Book of Questions"

and fills it with words of
pain and absence
sand and exile
love and loss.

Body

I have no idea what's going on inside me
I know I have a heart and kidneys and bones
and cell division and blood and veins
and that it's all busy and active
keeping me alive
yet I'm clueless nevertheless

What say do I really have in any of it?
Most of it just goes on anyway
and could just as well stop or malfunction
or breakdown or mutate
without checking with me first.

Time-Breath

Eventually you will run out
of time
Eventually you will no longer be able
to breathe.

Sleep

Each night I take all of me
all of my days
and this one just passed
and I lay myself down
and I enter the darkness
where I no longer need eyes to see
or legs to stand
where I no longer need to move through the world
where I am inert and deathly silent

My heart still beats
my veins still pulse
and time is ticking at my side
yet I am asleep to the world
hidden
like birds in the night
like the original darkness beyond the sun.

Rejuvenation

Everything made of wood or iron or flesh deteriorates
nothing lasts forever

Things grow old
the ages wear them down

Decay is inevitable
things need repair

The material requires rejuvenation
lest it rot and collapse around you

So too your soul
so too the people and things you love

They too require attention
repair
rejuvenation.

Reduction

Everything large reduces
Universe to galaxies
Galaxy to stars
Stars to planets
Planets to moon
Moon to earth
Earth to sky
Sky to horizon
Horizon to ocean
Ocean to waves
Waves to shore
Shore to sand
Sand to grains
And little creatures
And washed-up jelly fish
And me
Soon to die
Soon to return.

Once Upon a Time

Once upon a time
long ago
I lived

Six years old
twelve years old
thirty-three years old
fifty years old

Once upon a time
back then
I lived.

Living in the Present

It all depends on whether we measure time
from the beginning
or from the end

Does time gradually fade and erode
or does time come inescapably toward us?

Everything comes and goes

The future is always coming
The past is always receding

The gurus of our age tell us
Live in the present

To which I say
What choice do I have?
as though living in the present
were some sort of magic elixir

Yet surely the present also comes and goes.

You Who Are Passing

There are two ends
The entrance and the exit

How we enter is beyond our means
Only the end will show us
what we meant.

One Afternoon

Sometimes
an empty time comes upon me

The past feels lost
the future oblivious

All that is left
is this
empty time

This searing
Now.

Mortality

I am suspended
between heaven and earth

I am not sure whether to sink
or to rise.

Eternity

My body and my breath
keep me linked to time

When these are gone
so too is time.

Sundial

My sundial says
"The best is yet to be"

What a wonderful inscription
for a time-piece.

Gratitude

When I filter my existence through all its dim layers
When I am left with nothing except the wonder of it all
I find myself irresistibly drawn to give thanks and to praise

When I thank you
I become more aware of the need for your love in the world
and I try to be on your side.

4

Singularity

ON THE ONE HAND

I find rabbinic discussion intriguing because it is always "on the one hand, and on the other hand." They seem to know that life is innately "twofold" rather than "one and the same."

I have always tended to think in pairs. Does this mean I am a dualistic thinker? For example: science and religion, nature and society, justice and mercy, text and margin, you and me, God and humanity.

"Dualism," of course, is a word with bad press. No one wants to be called a dualistic thinker. Rather, it is better to be a holistic, integrated or non-dualistic thinker. Yet the rabbinic twofold-ness of life has always struck me as essential rather than dualistic. Life is always twofold—not duplicitous mind you, but twofold. There is always one and another. "I and Thou" as Martin Buber says: "the world is twofold in accordance with our twofold nature."

The main problem with dualistic thinking is that it makes one "pole" the master of the "other pole." Lopsided-ness occurs, oppression even, as one pole asserts dominance over the other—man over woman, society over nature, mind over matter.

I don't want anything to do with this type of dualistic thinking, which is why I prefer the word "relational" thinking. Two are always involved, and they shall never become "one"—especially not one over another. Rather, there is one *and* another, and no synthetic theme can merge or unify them. Only under such a condition is dialogue or relationship possible.

Making everything "One" is not the only way to undo or overcome dualistic thinking. There is always an other that escapes our need for integration. The alternative way is to see everything as relational—and there can be no relationship when everything is One rather than twofold.

In other words, twofold-ness can be conceived as relational rather than dualistic. What is the difference? Dualistic thought separates and then proceeds to dominate. Relational thought recognizes and then proceeds to engage.

Labeling is unhelpful. Are you a believer or a non-believer? Are you religious or secular? Are you conservative or progressive? Which pole do you subscribe to? The rabbis would find these questions farcical. Their basic principle is: "On the one hand, and on the other hand."

Are you a believer or a non-believer? Well, according to the rabbis, I am both. Sometimes I believe and I sometimes I don't. Are you good or evil? Again, according to the rabbis, I am both. I have the evil inclination (*yetzer ha-ra*) and the good inclination (*yetzer-ha-tov*).

It seems to me that, for the rabbis, there is a basic contestation happening all through life. It is always "on the one hand, and on the other hand." You may think this is a good thing, in the sense that it requires listening to all perspectives and then arriving at a resolution—yet the rabbis never reach a resolution or conclusion. It is always "on the one hand, on the other."

My own sense is that their insistence in maintaining a vigorous dialogue derives from their religious tradition that is rooted in monotheism. Theirs is not the pantheistic God who is One with Everything. Rather, theirs is the monotheistic God who is singular and unique—the one who cannot be encompassed or assimilated.

According to Jewish philosopher Abraham Heschel, "thinking and living can only be adequately understood in terms of a dialectic pattern, containing opposites or contrasted properties." There is a polarity at the heart of Judaism, a polarity that is like a magnet, and he gives examples such as uniformity and individuality, law and inwardness, love and fear, understanding and obedience, good and evil, time and eternity, revelation and response, empathy and self-expression, creed and faith—and, in his own words, "man's quest for God and God in search of man."[1]

---

1. Heschel, *God in Search of Man*, 341.

He goes so far as to suggest that "even God's relation to the world is characterized by the polarity of justice and mercy, providence and concealment, the promise of reward and the demand to serve Him for His sake." Judaism knows that there are always two hands: "on the one hand" and "on the other hand."

This attention to the twofold-ness of life aids us, paradoxically perhaps, to recognize or affirm that opposites are not necessarily mutually exclusive; they are often mutually required. As Heschel notes, "in actual living they involve each other." Twofold-ness means that two are needed and required. Our task, according to Heschel, is to learn to create harmony within our twofold existence. And yet this task is fraught with spiritual difficulty:

> Since each of the two principles moves in opposite direction, equilibrium can only be maintained if both are of equal force. But such a condition is rarely attained. Polarity is an essential trait of all things. Tension, contrast, and contradiction characterize all of reality. In the language of the *Zohar*, this world is called "the world of separation." Discrepancy, contention, ambiguity, and ambivalence afflict all of life, including the study of Torah . . .[2]

A SINGULAR LIFE

One of the oldest and most concentrated sayings in the Jewish tradition is the *Shema:* "Hear O Israel. The Lord our God, the Lord is one" (Deut 6:4). Along with its appeal that we listen, the *Shema* reminds us that God is "one" (*ehad*) and like no other. So too, each and every person who is made in God's image is "one" and like no other. *Ehad* means "unique" or "only" like the etymology of the English word "only" is "one-ly." In this sense, the one is the *singular one* rather than the unifying or *all-embracing one.*

A Talmudic passage uses the image of minting coins. Whereas human beings strike coins with the same die and gets coins all alike, the Holy One strikes each person with the die of Adam, and not one is the same as another. Human beings are not like minted coins, interchangeable and alike. Rather, human beings are incomparable and unique. This incomparableness reveals "the trace of God" in humanity.[3] Each person's

---

2. Heschel, *God in Search of Man*, 341–42.
3. Levinas, *Outside the Subject*, 118.

existence is holy and irreplaceable because each person is made in the image of God who is holy and like no other.

Every life is a life of singular uniqueness. Every death is a death of a singular uniqueness. Life and death are singular events. It is almost impossible to "universalize" or "encompass" them, without somehow denying or overcoming their unique existence.

To know that God is one is to know that every created being is born in this singular image, rather than in the image of "all-ness." If we speak of human dignity, for example, then surely we are speaking of a unique and special one rather than a unified or collectivized One.

Even though we are only here once—or maybe because we are only here once—our lives on earth are heavy with consequences that can never be cancelled. "Whatever you bind on earth will be bound in heaven, and whatever you release on earth will be released in heaven" (Matt 18:18). The deeds we perform may seem slight, yet they carry consequences that affect the lives of those around us, and maybe even the lives of those distant to us. Our actions and words are not performed or spoken in a vacuum or a void. They can do good or harm; they can bind or release; they bear responsibility; they carry the weight of good and evil.

AN APPLE

A living parable:

> Slice an apple through its equator, and you will find five small chambers arrayed in a perfectly symmetrical starburst—a pentagram. Each of the chambers holds a seed (occasionally two) of such deep lustrous brown they might have been oiled and polished by a woodworker . . .
>
> Every seed in that apple . . . contains the genetic instructions for a completely new and different apple tree, one that, if planted, would bear only the most glancing resemblance to its parents. If not for grafting—the ancient technique for cloning trees—every apple in the world would be its own distinct variety, and it would be impossible to keep a good one going beyond the life span of that particular tree.
>
> The botanical term for this variability is "heterozygosity," and while there are many species that share it (our own included), in the apple the tendency is extreme. More than any other single trait, it is the apple's genetic variability—its ineluctable wildness—that

accounts for its ability to make itself at home in places as different from one another as New England, New Zealand, Kazakhstan and California. Wherever the apple tree goes, its offspring propose so many different variations on what it means to be an apple—at least five per apple, several thousand per tree—that a couple of these novelties are almost bound to have whatever qualities it takes to prosper in the tree's adopted home.[4]

This living parable is a celebration of life's inherent plurality, diversity and variety—its "ineluctable wildness."

Can we imagine that God, like an artist in rapture, could be so wildly superfluous as to allow several thousand distinct varieties of apples to emerge from a single tree—each one never to be repeated?

"God said, 'Let the earth produce . . .'" (Gen 1.11). "God said, 'Be fruitful, multiply . . .'" (1:22). "God saw that it was good" (Gen 1:25). Better that life be full and rich and many and assorted, rather than uniform, identical, limited, one and the same.

Apples and humans, we are told, are "heterozygous." We are distinct and we are plural. We are unique and we are diverse. We do not emerge as mere replicas that are one and the same—a homogeneous mass. Rather, we burst forth as diverse and different—a heterogeneous flourishing.

God colors all creation with a radiant heterogeneity—"the thousands of different languages spoken by humanity, the proliferation of cultures, the sheer variety of the imaginative expressions of the human spirit, in most of which, if we listen carefully, we will hear the voice of wisdom telling us something we need to know."[5]

This astonishing multiplicity does not mean we are disparate and isolated from each other or from our fellow living creatures who share the earth. Rather, it means we are inseparable and interconnected, bound and woven by the creative energy of God who has fashioned us to thrive like apple trees.

---

4. Pollan, *The Botany of Desire*, 10–11.
5. Sacks, *The Dignity of Difference*, 20–21.

Love at First Sight

You can't go past
love at first sight

Everything else
is simply deliberation
and procrastination.

Incomparable

The one thing you cannot do is compare

As soon as you compare something
it loses its singularity

"All comparison injures"
Kierkegaard says
"It is an evil."

Unique

Everyone is unique, exceptional, unprecedented

Now, try building a society on this basis

No chance

Yet this is what "as it is in heaven" means.

The Singular

My existence
God's existence
A Tree's existence
Your existence.

New Life

When life comes into the world
it is brand new
it is pure future-tense.

Holiness

True holiness hallows everything
such that there is no
religious standpoint.

Birds

Phenomenology means "letting things appear"

This requires silence and stillness
so that wild and original life
is not frightened away.

Singularities

Singularities are not fragmented jumbles
of inarticulate and unsystematised life

They are the very "things" that allow access
to the universal dimensions of God's love

"In so far as you did this to one of the least . . . "

Personal

The personal is the reason for the public
rather than its antithesis

An impersonal society
is no society at all.

Love Your Neighbour

The command to love your neighbour
is not a realm of knowledge beyond your reach
but a teaching that teaches you
what is possible.

In Between

I'm always working on two things
at the same time

love and hate
justice and mercy
life and death
you and me

I'm in between.

Life in Two Halves

The institutional
the administrative
the impersonal
and
the relational
the dialogical
the unique.

Distance

You are far, far away
you are miles and miles away from me

You don't even exist
you are that far

You are like a tiny spec on the horizon
like cows grazing way up on the hills

Why this distance between us?

Incarnation

I want real

Real body
Real flesh
Real eyes
Real skin

I don't want the world of theories and ideas
I want you here
Now
With your clothes falling off
Your bra unclipped
Your nakedness

This is what I want

Fact
Flesh
Body.

A Million and One Truths

I don't see how we can get a million and one truths
all wrapped-up into One.

Love is Possible

Separation is possible
even in the deepest love

Distance is possible
even in the closest love

Unknowing is possible
even in the truest love.

I love Love

I love that I can love God
I love that I can love the moon
I love that I can love you

I love that I can love

The interior world is no match
for exteriority.

5

Natural Lover

NATURAL LOVER

Creation is God's first and primary gift to us. I don't know if there is a better exemplar of creativity than nature itself. Everything in nature tends toward creation and life.

Indigenous cultures have long known and celebrated this. I imagine that the first sounds of music came from listening to nature's symphony—the singing of birds, the humming of cicadas, the roar of the ocean—string, woodwind and base.

Of all the ways that God is revealed, nature is the most majestic. Nature can turn death into life. Nature can create whole new beings. Nature can live without fear of dying. There is a divine power in nature. The demonic is more likely to appear in human societies.

Is nature simply the cycle of birth and death, repeated infinitely? When I look at the natural world, I do not see death happening around me; I see life happening around me. Nature's great miracle is that it continually renews itself as a great energy towards life.

We are here for life and for love; we are not here for death. Biological or cyclical understandings of life are not the full picture, as though life simply arises and then rots on the forest floor. There are many people who face the spectre of death in their lives through poverty and conflict, and we can't simply look at them and say, "Oh well, that's just nature's way." Rather, we are called to be concerned for the death that often comes violently or prematurely to others, that inflicts others.

There is a moral and vital "law of life" that pervades the universe and it is the human vocation to align their lives with this creative goodness. It is a profound affirmation, a *yes* to life and to the holiness of life. In the mystical tradition this is known as the experience of *kataphasis*—affirmation, wonder, giving thanks, and speaking-with rather than against life's goodness and beauty. It is a great *Amen,* to the world and to humanity, and to God who affirms and sustains all existence.

Genesis

Genesis
is a most appropriate name
for the first book of the Bible

In the beginning
God did not create religion
God created the world.

Natural Lover

I was born this way
I had no choice
I was born to be a natural lover.

The Song of Birds

Who really listens?

The other day
the president of America
the world's most powerful man
gave a press conference
in the Rose Garden
on a sunny, Spring day
in Washington DC
thronged by reporters
ABC, NBC, CNN
Yet all I could hear
amidst and beneath and over the top
was the sound of singing birds
beautifully and blissfully chirping
in the Rose Garden.

No Regulation

Rules are a sign
that society can't behave
naturally.

Moon

Amidst all the wonders of our world
the moon begins
frail
fragile
just a scrape
then rises
grows
full-bodied
wide-eyed
and in horror
seeing it all
shrinks back
frail
fragile
and disappears.

The Ecliptic

Stretched out before me tonight
is a beautiful view of the arc of the planets

Mars rising in the east
The moon ahead by a few hours
Jupiter on the high bend of the arc
Venus setting in the West

A perfect alignment of moon and planets
travelling the ecliptic arc

Yet my life at the moment feels very non-aligned
I have lost my path, my trajectory
the arc of my existence

The universe teaches me that when I am skewed or out of alignment
I need to seek again the ecliptic path
of my own life.

The Big Love Theory

This is not a scientific theory
This is a religious theory

It is a religious theory, not because it is about religion
Rather, it is derived from God

This theory says, everything radiates from God's Great Heart
Everything burns with God's Great Love

The universe is Big Love
Large love
Expansive love

We may find ourselves feeling very small
infinitesimal
Yet we are held in the arms of a big universe and a big love

This is the Big Love Theory.

The Elements

Maybe the Greeks had it right
when they named the elements

Earth
Wind
Fire
Water

The only thing I would add is
Soul.

Mystery and Majesty

In mystery you are lost to me
In majesty you are revealed.

The Revelation of the Moon

Our life is like the moon
I suppose we could say that it is also like the sun
Both rise and set

Yet I've never known a half-sun
The sun is always full

The moon, however, takes time before it attains fullness
The moon takes shape like a pregnant belly
It takes time to become fully round

Our life is like the moon
New, like a scrape of silver on the horizon
Growing larger and larger each night
Until the whole night sky is cast in glowing white light
Then shrinking, hiding again
Fading into radiant starlight
The sky deep and dark

I've never seen the sun do the same
Except maybe for glorious orange sunsets
Or fresh morning rays
Yet nothing quite like the moon

Unabashed
Traveling the night sky
The moon lets me gaze upon it
And seems unafraid of revealing itself to me.

Solar System

I felt the sun's warmth
touch my naked skin

I felt the furnace
of a burning star.

Galileo

The earth is spinning and revolving
We live in great, swirling arcs
around the sun
on the tail-end of a spiraling galaxy

Unique—a small, blue planet
dot-point in a vast cosmos
This life—given here and now
centre-point of the universe

Among the billions of galaxies
earth nevertheless stands unique
as though all of creation
and this small blue planet
were made for us
as a great gift from God.

Star Maps

It must have been a marvel
to discover the patterns and pathways
of the night sky

To be guided by their faithful reference points
constants
amidst change.

Earth Rise

For millennia we watched the sun and the moon rise

                        It was only in the nineteen-sixties
                                 that we also saw
                                       the earth rise.

Dwelling

There is no uninhabited place
no vacuum or void
no inhospitality

Everything dwells
in the presence of an other.

The Jewish Day Begins at Night

When you wake in the morning
memory is the first thing that confronts you

When you sleep at night
future is the first thing that awaits you

The early morning sun is filled with the past
The late rising moon is filled with the future

This is the logic of those who build their calendars
around the moon
such that a new day begins at night.

Birds of the Pond

I longed to say to the birds
(always wary)
"Don't be afraid of me. I love you!"

I imagine that God has the same thought
toward me.

The Wind is Back

The wind roams the hilltops
like a vagabond
like a spirit
blowing toward me
and rushing away.

Nudgee Beach

You promised me that my tide would come in
yet today you showed me the tidal flats
the ocean withdrawing into itself.

Evolution

The mangrove tree learnt to send its roots up
rather than down.

If We Could Be Human

If we could be like bees
we would sip honey from as many flowers as possible

If we could be like birds
we would trust the wind and the currents of the air

If we could be like trees
we would sink our roots and spread our branches

If we could be like humans
we would give ourselves into each other's care.

Regulation-Free Zone

This land is a regulation free zone
There is only God's law
a natural law
in a natural environment.

Untamed

I love birds
especially when they draw close
displaying amazing trust
across the barrier of our strangeness
as though some primal part of them
recognized creation's friendship

I love this capacity for friendship
expressed in the wild and the untamed.

A Natural Theologian

Is it any wonder that
a theologian
would love birds
and books
and people
and stars.

Working the Land

I work the land
and the land works me

Let the land love you
let the land heal you

Let the land teach you
let the land be

It's too cool for school
it cannot be taught

It is the lesson
only the land can teach.

Hinterland

A ridge of life
between
the escarpments
and the ocean

A state of being
margin of land
margin of life
Hinterland.

Full Moon

How could you ever be dishonest or untrue
under the radiance of a full moon?

Infinite

Under a brilliant night sky
the infinite takes over.

The Wind

The wind is the most naked body.

Natural Divinity

I've always loved nature
like I've always loved God

Yet I know that nature and God are not the same
Nature is God's artistry.

Evolution

There is something in your eyes
Where did it come from?
a spark
a window
a glistening
There is something in your eyes
How did it get there?

6

Desire

REPETITION—HOW THE LOVE OF GOD NEEDS TO BE LEARNT OVER AND OVER AGAIN

Repetition is common in many religious traditions; for example, in liturgical rituals and cycles of readings. It is rare that great teachings are learnt on one reading alone. They often need to be repeated.

The early rabbinic teachers were known as "repeaters" (*Tannaim*). Repetition is required for all learning. Very few people learn things "once and for all." Rather, their learning is many times over.

Repetition need not be a bad thing. It can also help us attend, over and over again, to the very thing we are trying to learn and to practice.

Philosopher and Tamludic commentator Emmanuel Levinas repeats many of his key themes in various ways throughout his works: "Love your neighbor. Love God. There is no one without the other."

He is a "repeater" of tradition and stands in a long line of repeaters: "Hear, O Israel . . . repeat these words . . ." (Deut 6:7).

Repetition is a form of concentration. For example, I have sat with the following verse over many months: "One cannot serve two masters" (Matt 6:24).

This verse has now seeped into my being. The temptation of serving two masters has grown weaker and weaker, such that I realize it is only one master I can serve. The repetition of this verse has aided my realization of it.

Recently, a new verse captured my attention: "Unless the Lord builds the house, the builders labor in vain" (Psalm 127:1).

There is much to be learnt from this verse. The other day, however, I was surprised even further when the second verse was brought to my attention:

> In vain you rise early
> and stay up late,
> for the Lord grants sleep to those he loves.

This verse has been especially important for me during the past few weeks as I have grappled with anxiety and insomnia. I repeat it as I sleep.

GLOWING COALS

Rabbinic commentary is compared to glowing coals—"the words of the sages are like glowing embers." Why embers? Why not a flame? "Because it only becomes a flame when one learns to blow on it." One must blow on the embers so that the flame arises. "The coals light up by being blown on, the glow of the flame that thus comes alive depends on the interpreter's length of breath."[1]

THE MIND IS AN EXCELLENT SERVANT

I read a quote recently that has stayed with me, though I can't remember now where I read it. It goes like this: "The mind is an excellent servant but a terrible master."

I have spent the last few nights turning in my bed, my mind caught-up in anxieties, invading my night. I can relate to the second-half of the quote: "the mind is a terrible master." When our mind masters us, we enter all sorts of terrible worlds—depression or anxiety, yet also egoism and delusional power. A mastering mind leads to all sorts of terrible outcomes—fundamentalism, dogmatism, authoritarianism.

A mastering mind is not what we want or need. What we need is a servant mind, which is the beginning of the quote: "the mind is an excellent servant." A servant mind is unafraid to lose control, unafraid to follow the question, unafraid to serve rather than to master.

---

1. Levinas, *Beyond the Verse,* 210.

A servant mind is not anxious to know-it-all. What it loses in terms of mastery, it gains in terms of openness and discovery. What it loses in terms of control and security, it gains in terms of mystery and majesty. A servant mind is an excellent mind.

Existentialism

Finally
a school of philosophy
born of feeling
rather than ideas

Anxiety
or better
Desire
or worse
Dread.

Enlightenment

1.00am
2.00am
3.00am

The dog barks
The moon shines
The floorboards creak

Restlessness
Insomnia
Wakefulness

Everything is dark
The whole world is asleep
Yet there is always one who is awake.

As Though It Might Go Away

The feeling of abandonment
of radical discontent

It is pointless
to seek release from this

As though it were simply a disturbance
that might go away

Or a trial
that might end one day

This fault
this rift
this tear.

Tikkun

The shattered vessels
that contain God's light
can always be repaired

The damage done
and the damage we do
can always be repaired.

Surrender

It takes a long
long
long
long
long
long
time
to let go.

So Real and So True

What do I do
when I know something
is so real
and so true
yet I am unable
to realize it?

Exile

I don't understand why I am cut-off
sitting on the banks of Babylon
dreaming of Jerusalem.

Incarnation

For every lofty idea
you need a lowly idea

For every hope and aspiration
you need a circumstance and situation

For every spirit that rises
you need a spirit made flesh.

Believing

If you believe in love and goodness
it is inevitable that you will suffer
affliction.

Awake

Awake: the Enlightened One
Insomnia: the Troubled One.

Love and Fear

We can often be afraid of love
afraid of love's gifts and requirements
preferring instead
the world of fear and anxiety.

Non-Attachment

It's not about
non-attachment

It's about the right type
of attachment.

Desire

Desire takes a bit of sorting
because not all desire is good

It may simply be envy
or addiction
or craziness.

Purify Your Desire

Desire less or
desire more

What part of my desire
must increase
and what part decrease?

Extinguishing the Flame

Don't kid yourself
desire never ends

Without it
no flame arises.

Even When You Run

Even when you run
even when you drive your car

Still
you're alone

Even when you sit on your couch
even when you drink your wine

Still
you're alone

Even when you dream
even when you try and try and try

Still
you're alone

Existence is ruthless
stripping you bare

till nothing is left
but you alone.

On Tap

Give me that and
give me that as well
I want it all on tap

I don't wanna wait
till tomorrow
I don't wanna wait
for you
I don't wanna hold back
I want it all on tap

Give it to me now
no point waiting anymore
Give it to me while you can
no point holding off
Give it to me pure and neat
no point mixing it up

I want it straight
I want it direct
I want it all on tap.

When I was Young

When I was young
you made me feel that
nothing would be perfect
without you

Now I am old
very little has changed.

Life

You must live the necessities
and the requirements

Yet you also need the joy
and the releasement.

Self-Help

Sometimes
I just can't help myself

No matter how hard I try
I just can't help myself.

The Path

I don't need to find
a new path

I'm happy to travel the path
I've always been on.

Do What You Love

Do what you love
This is your best antidote
to doing what you hate.

Head and Heart

Thought will only take you so far
Heart will take you
all the way.

Spirit

You really don't know from whence it comes
or where it goes
So you stammer and you gasp and you cry and you love
but you never really know

"Does it bother you that you don't know?"

"No, not anymore."

Everything Begins with Feeling

> You can't think God
> but you can feel God
>
> You can't think love
> but you can feel love
>
> Everything begins with feeling.

Sacred Heart

An antique image
yet surely a suffering and burning heart
is aflame in us all?

Tenderness

Do not think it is foolish
or naïve
to believe that
we can be tender
with all things.

The Test of Love

The crucial test
you can apply to anything
is the test of love

Yet there are those who say
this is just pure romanticism
as though the test of love
were no test at all.

Do Not Worry About Your Life

I know things didn't work out too well today

                                        That's all right
                              Don't let it get you down

               I know you have doubts and regrets and
                      things you wish you could change

                                        That's all right
                              Don't let it get you down

                                I know you come home
                                and drink your wine
                                and try to forget

                                          That's all right
                              Don't let it get you down

                                Things will work out
                                     It will be OK
                                Don't worry too much

                            You can only do a little bit
                                  you can't do it all

                When you feel yourself crumbling
                                              wasted
                                      and spent

                            Don't let it get you down
                Don't let it get the better of you.

Prayer

I want to love the world
and I want the world to love me
but it's way out of my hands

I want to love you
and I want you to love me
but it's way out of my control

I want to love and be loved
but it's virtually impossible.

Wounded Heart

I cannot stand it when my
heart is wounded

It is my heart I need most
and I hate to see it suffer

To wound another's heart
is the cruelest of evils

Our hearts are all we have
to keep us alive.

Thank You

I want to thank you
even though I am not sure
you are there

Yet somehow when I thank you
I feel your presence
more and more.

L'Chaim

Affirmation is one of the most amazing forces in the universe

To life
For life

It is the elixir par excellence.

Needing Love

Sometimes
when you need love
there is an underlying current
that warns and cautions you

Do not let this current stop you.

In Love

Take a chance with love

Get out of something
or get into something
but decide.

Free at Last

I want to be like St Francis
in the forest of peace

I want to be like St Therese
the little flower

I want to be like Julian of Norwich
All will be well

I want to be like MLK
Free at last!

7

You/Divinity

YOU AND I AGAIN

Why speak about "you"? After all, what do I know, what could I say, what could I possibly write about you?

Perhaps, instead, I should be writing about me? An autobiography?

Or, at least, an exercise of writing that realizes that nothing can be written about you that isn't, in the first place, situated and contextualized within the framework of "me"—my culture, my context, my perspective. It seems I cannot know much about you at all—just the little bits and pieces that come filtered through the predominance of my "self" and my "worldview."

Yet don't you want to be known? Or do you fear that I will simply appropriate you, that everything I know about you will be according to "my take on things," that I won't really allow you to be you? Perhaps you prefer to keep your distance from me, to preserve your own distinct otherness, to be *you* in your own right. Yet it seems like such a sad state of affairs—me over here, and you over there—and never the twain shall meet.

Do you really want to remain alone, unreachable, hidden? Wouldn't it be rather arrogant of you to claim this specialized preserve, this place of supreme "un-knowability"? If you really want to remain unknown and unknowable, then why do I bother with you? Better to leave you alone.

Or are you all the time reaching out and saying who you are, speaking to me and trying to get my attention? As though you really *do* want to be known and loved?

Is my desire to know you such a bad thing? Am I not honoring you when I say that I want to know you? And if I write about you, isn't this better than just writing about myself? And if I love you, isn't this better than just loving myself? Besides, you are always there anyway. I don't know of any time in my life when I am purely "myself." It is not self-possession or self-knowledge that I seek. Rather, I want to know you.

When I speak about knowing you, I mean more than simply knowledge. I mean that form of knowing that is filled with the essentiality of love. Maybe this is what you are trying to tell me—that in all my efforts to know you—it is really you who knows me, who sees me, who loves me? Maybe I have it all wrong—the wrong direction—it is not "from me to you." Rather, it is "from you to me."

I and You

There is nothing more practical
or spiritual
than a relationship.

God

It is very easy to tell
whether or not another exists.

God-Incidences

It was a random meeting
a beggar on the street

"There are no co-incidences," she said
only "God-incidences."

The Task

I didn't think the task I had set myself would be this difficult
I didn't think I would have to grapple with it day after day
I didn't think it would be this demanding

What task?

To trust God's love.

Belief

It's nice knowing
that you're there.

God is Dead

"We have killed God"
What a strange remark

I sit and ponder the moon and the stars
on this lonely beach

I sit among the limitless
and feel my own substance dying
feel my own life outstripped

I cannot conceive that God is dead
or that it is within our power
to utter such words

Rather
there is nothing
facing God
that can live.

Infinitesimal

My smallness does not diminish me
It is a natural correlate
of God's vastness.

Always There

Can I attempt a time without you
Can I move away from you
Can I leave you behind, leave you out
Can I expunge you from my existence?

You are There

You are inside
They say
You are deeply buried within me
They say
You are hidden somewhere in my body they say
Somewhere in my heart
Or in my soul
Or in my memory
Or in my desire

Somewhere
You are inside of me
They say

And so I look for you
Inside of me
Inside my heart
Inside my head
Inside my arms
Inside my legs
Inside my blood
Inside my veins
Somewhere they say
You are inside of me

But then I wonder
After years of trying to find you
Whether you are really there
Inside of me
As they say

Maybe you are elsewhere
Maybe you are outside of me
Not inside, but outside
Not a deeply buried mystery within me
But a wondrously existing presence
Outside of me

Maybe you are out there
Somewhere?

Not me
You.

Addict

To whom else can I go?
you hold the keys
to eternal life

To whom else can I turn?
you are always there
over and over again

What point is there?
trying to escape
trying to pretend

that my life could go on
without you.

Inescapability

I know you've laid a trap for me
Yet it doesn't worry me anymore
I almost expect it

You catch me
You hold me
You won't let me go.

Them

Why do I worry about them
when all I really want
is you.

Covenant

"I promise if you promise"

That's about as close as we can get
to unconditional love.

God

God will never say
"It's over"
Only we can.

Holding on to You

I remember being so close to you
I remember holding on to you

I don't know why
and I don't know when

but somewhere along the track
I let go of you.

If I Don't Make It (VM)

If I don't make it through the week
if I don't make it through the day
can you come and be with me?

If I don't make it through the night
if I don't make it here and now
can you come and rescue me?

If it all goes down
and nothing is left standing
can you come and hold me up?

If I am just here
just now
just like this
can you come and see me through?

Your Ways Are Not My Ways

You give me this
but you don't give me that

I guess you are trying to tell me
something.

Ships in the Night

We are like ships in the night
afloat on an immense ocean
under a vast night sky

Occasionally we pass one another
and draw comfort
that we are not alone.

Another Will

You know there is another will
when you go into the ocean
and you realize that the waves
have got the better of you.

Belief

Let me tell you what belief does

It doesn't turn you into a fanatic
It doesn't mean you are out of your mind
It doesn't stop all your fears and doubts

Belief is the attempt
to stay in agreement with life.

Will Power

I wish that will power had nothing to do
with loving God

I wish that I were rather overcome
and could not but surrender.

Jeremiah

"You have seduced me
and I have let myself be seduced."

Losing the Power to Say "I"

I abdicate
I renounce myself
I relinquish my power to say
"I"

I have
no choice
I am
defeated

You, You
always You
whenever I flee the ruins

I surrender
Thou art greater than I am.

God

Is it really true?
Not simply that God exists
but something even more unfathomable
that God is love.

The Other Day

The other day she kept interrupting me

I was droning on and on
and she kept interrupting me

I went everywhere
down to the depths
up to the heights

But she kept interrupting me

I said it all
as best I could
the good and the bad
the great and the small

But she kept interrupting me

She kept coming back
again and again
like a broken record
like she didn't really care
what I was saying

Interrupting me
interjecting
constantly
continually
asserting
enforcing even

"I love you"

It was a totally bewildering experience.

My Paradox

Alone
with You.

Transcendence

Transcendence—the bridge
Immanence—the shores.

Consolation

You console me
and soothe my soul
You bathe me in your love
and teach me: "All will be well"

You take away my worries
and show me the birds
You lift me up and say
"It will be alright"

You carry me on your shoulders
and look for me when I am lost
You bring me great consolation
leaving 99 behind

You search me out
and know my soul.

No End to Loving You

I loved you then
I love you now
I can't imagine why
it would ever change

Old love
yet loving you still
as though there were no end
to loving you.

The Expanding File

Bibliography

Alves, Rubem. *The Poet, The Warrior, The Prophet*. London: SCM, 1990.
Berdyaev, Nikolai. *Slavery and Freedom*. Translated by R.M. French. New York: Charles Scribner's Sons, 1944.
Blanchot, Maurice. *The Writing of the Disaster*. Translated by Ann Smock. Lincoln and London: University of Nebraska Press, 1995.
Brueggemann, Walter. *Hope Within History*. Atlanta: John Knox, 1987.
Buber, Martin. *I and Thou*. Translated by Walter Kaufmann. Edinburgh: T & T Clark, 1970.
Cash, Johhny. *American V: A Hundred Highways*. CD. Sony Music, 2006.
Celan, Paul. *Selected Poems and Prose of Paul Celan*. Translated by John Felstiner. New York: W. W. Norton, 2001.
Chardin, Teilhard de. *The Divine Milieu*. New York: Harper & Row/Perennial, 1960.
Cohen, Leonard. "Avalanche." In *Stranger Music: Selected Poems and Songs*. New York: Vintage Books, 1993.
———. "Everybody Knows." In *Stranger Music: Selected Poems and Songs*. New York: Vintage Books, 1993.
Day, Dorothy. *The Duty of Delight: The Diaries of Dorothy Day*. Edited by Robert Ellsberg. New York: Image Books, 2008.
Edgerton, W. Dow. *The Passion of Interpretation*. Louisville, Kentucky: Westminster/John Knox Press, 1992.
Ferguson, Margaret, and Mary Jo Salter, Jon Stallworthy, eds. *The Norton Anthology of Poetry*. New York: W. W. Norton, 1996.
Forché, Carolyn, ed. *Against Forgetting: Twentieth-Century Poetry of Witness*. New York: W. W. Norton, 1993.
Freire, Paulo. *Pedagogy of the Oppressed*. Ringwood, Victoria: Penguin Books, 1972.
Heaney, Seamus. *The Redress of Poetry*. London: Faber and Faber, 1995.
Heidegger, Martin. *Poetry, Language, Thought*. Translated by Albert Hofstadter. New York: Harper & Row/Perennial, 1971.
Heschel, Abraham. *God in Search of Man: A Philosophy of Judaism*. New York: Farrar, Straus and Giroux, 1951.
———. *Heavenly Torah: As Refracted through the Generations*. Edited and translated by Gordon Tucker with Leonard Levin. New York: Continuum, 2010.
———. *Who is Man?* Stanford: Stanford University Press, 1965.
Jabés, Edmond. *The Book of Questions*. Published in 2 volumes. Translated by Rosmarie Waldrop. Hanover, N.H.: University Press of New England/Wesleyan University Press, 1972/1983.

———. *The Book of Resemblances*. Translated by Rosmarie Waldrop. Hanover, N.H.: University Press of New England/Wesleyan University Press, 1990.
Kaufman, Walter. "I and You: A Prologue." In Martin Buber, *I and Thou*. Translated by Walter Kaufmann. Edinburgh: T & T Clark, 1970.
Keefe-Perry, L. Callid. *Way to Water: A Theopoetics Primer*. Eugene: Oregon: Cascade Books, 2014.
Kohak, Erazim. *The Embers and the Stars: A Philosophical Inquiry into the Moral Sense of Nature*. Chicago: University of Chicago Press, 1984.
Kushner, Lawrence. *The Book of Letters: a Mystical Alef-bait*. Woodstock, Vermont: Jewish Lights, 1990.
Kwasny, Melissa, ed. *Toward the Open Field: Poets on the Art of Poetry*. Middletown, Connecticut: Wesleyan University Press, 2004.
Leclercq, Jean. *The Love of Learning and the Desire for God*. New York: Fordham University Press, 1961.
Lee, Bernard. *Jesus and the Metaphors of God: The Christs of the New Testament*. New York: Paulist, 1993.
Levinas, Emmanuel. *Alterity and Transcendence*. Translated by Michael B. Smith. New York: Columbia University Press, 1999.
———. *Entre Nous: Thinking-of-the-Other*. Translated by Michael B. Smith and Barbara Harshav. New York: Columbia University Press, 1998.
———. *In the Time of the Nations*. Translated by Michael B. Smith. London: Continuum, 2007.
———. "Interview with Emmanuel Levinas." Edith Wyschogrod. *Philosophy & Theology* 4 (1989): 105–18.
———. *Is It Righteous to Be? Interviews with Emmanuel Levinas*. Edited by Jill Robins. Stanford: Stanford University Press, 2001.
———. *Outside the Subject*. Translated by Michael B. Smith. Stanford: Stanford University Press, 1993.
Macmurray, John. *Reason and Emotion*. London: Faber & Faber, 1992.
Maritain, Jacques. *Creative Intuition in Art and Poetry*. New York: Pantheon Books, 1953.
Matt, Daniel. *The Essential Kabbalah*. San Francisco: HarperSanFrancisco, 1996.
Meland, Bernard. "The Appreciative Consciousness." In *Higher Education and the Human Spirit*. Chicago: Chicago University Press, 1953.
Menkhorst, Peter, et al. *The Australian Bird Guide*. Clayton, South Victoria: CSIRO, 2017.
Merton, Thomas. *Silence in Heaven: A Book of Monastic Life*. London: Thames and Hudson, 1956.
Morrison, Van. "Rave On, John Donne." In *Lit Up Inside: Selected Lyrics*. Edited by Eamonn Hughes. London: Faber & Faber, 2014.
———. "See Me Through." In *Lit Up Inside: Selected Lyrics*. Edited by Eamonn Hughes. London: Faber & Faber, 2014.
Pollan, Michael. *The Botany of Desire: A Plant's-Eye View of the World*. New York: Random House, 2001.
Rahner, Karl. "Poetry and the Christian." In *Theological Investigations* 4. New York: Darton, Longman & Todd, 1975.
Rich, Adrienne. *What is Found There: Notebooks on Poetry and Politics*. London: Virago, 1993.
Ricoeur, Paul. *Living Up To Death*. Chicago: University of Chicago Press, 2009.

———. *The Symbolism of Evil*. Translated by Emerson Buchanan. Boston: Beacon Press, 1967.

Rilke, Rainer Maria. *Rilke's Book of Hours*. Translated by Anita Barrows and Joanna Macy. New York: Riverhead Books, 1996.

Sacks, Jonathan. *The Dignity of Difference: How to Avoid the Clash of Civilizations*. London: Continuum, 2002.

Schreiter, Robert. *The Ministry of Reconciliation*. Maryknoll: Orbis Books, 1998.

Soelle, Dorothee. *The Mystery of Death*. Minneapolis: Fortress, 2007.

———. *The Silent Cry: Mysticism and Resistance*. Minneapolis: Fortress, 2001.

Steiner, George. *Real Presences*. Chicago: University of Chicago Press, 1989.

Thompson, Gregg D. *The Australian Guide to Stargazing*. Sydney: New Holland, 2001.

Tracy, David. *The Analogical Imagination: Christian Theology and the Pluralism of Cultures*. New York: Crossroad, 1981.

Veling, Terry A. *For You Alone: Emmanuel Levinas and the Answerable Life*. Eugene, Oregon: Cascade Books, 2014.

———. "The Personal and Spiritual Life: All Too Human, All Too Divine." *The Way* 52 (2013) 7–21.

———. "Poetic License." *International Journal of Practical Theology* 23.1 (2019) 39–48.

———. *Spiral-Bound Poetry*. Santiago: Hebel Ediciones, 2014.

www.ingramcontent.com/pod-product-compliance
Lightning Source LLC
Chambersburg PA
CBHW062008220426
43662CB00010B/1272